PRAYERS

~ OF ~

✦INTERCESSION✦

FOR COMMON WORSHIP

PRAYERS

~ OF ~

INTERCESSION

FOR COMMON WORSHIP

SUSAN SAYERS

Kevin
Mayhew

This edition published in 1999 by
KEVIN MAYHEW LTD
Buxhall
Stowmarket
Suffolk IP14 3BW

Reprinted 2002

Prayers of Intercession for Common Worship is extracted from
Living Stones – Prayers of Intercession, Years A, B and C.

ISBN 1 84003 473 4
Catalogue No. 1500321

Cover design by Jaquetta Sergeant
Edited by Peter Dainty
Typesetting by Kevin Whomes

Printed and Bound in Great Britain

FOREWORD

A praying church is a living organism, powered by the love of God, and directed by his will. The aim of those leading intercessions in public worship is to provide a suitable climate for prayer, both for the faithful core of praying members, and also for those who drift in as visitors, sometimes willingly and sometimes rather grudgingly.

Since our God is in a far better position to know the needs of each muddle of people who arrive on any particular Sunday, it is obviously sensible to prepare for leading the intercessions by praying for those who will be there, asking our God to lead us with his agenda in mind, rather than taking immediate charge ourselves. Then we have to give him a chance to answer! You may find that a quiet walk enables you to do this, or a time wandering round the empty church, or time spent on some of the mechanical jobs at home while you still your heart and resist the temptation to badger God with good ideas.

I have provided ideas to reflect the day's readings, and as you read through them you may well find that these ideas will spark off other thoughts of your own. Do use them however you wish – exactly as they stand, adapted to suit specific needs, or simply as a starting point. They are a resource to help you, not a cage to keep your own ideas out.

During the service be alert to what is being said and how God is moving among you, so that you can pick up on these threads, if it seems appropriate, during the intercessions. And if you have young children present, give some thought to how they can also be praying at this time. They might be following a picture prayer trail, singing a quiet worship song, drawing some situation they are praying for, or looking through the intercession pictures provided in children's communion books, such as *Jesus is Here* (Kevin Mayhew, 1993).

I have heard it said that since God can hear the prayers, it doesn't really matter if the congregation can't. I don't agree. In public worship it can be very distracting to be straining to hear, or isolating if you can hear only a vague mumble. Do take the trouble to practise speaking clearly and fairly slowly in the church, so that everyone can comfortably take in what you are saying. Bear in mind that nerves usually make us speed up somewhat, so speak extra slowly to allow for this.

Finally, don't recite what you have written, but pray it. Pray it both through the intentions and through the silences. Leading the intercessions carries a great responsibility, but it is also a great privilege.

SUSAN SAYERS

CONTENTS

	Year A	Year B	Year C
ADVENT			
First Sunday of Advent	12	134	256
Second Sunday of Advent	14	136	258
Third Sunday of Advent	16	138	260
Fourth Sunday of Advent	18	140	262
CHRISTMAS			
Christmas Day	20	142	264
First Sunday of Christmas	22	144	266
Second Sunday of Christmas	24	146	268
EPIPHANY			
The Epiphany	26	148	270
The Baptism of Christ:			
First Sunday of Epiphany	28	150	272
Second Sunday of Epiphany	30	152	274
Third Sunday of Epiphany	32	154	276
Fourth Sunday of Epiphany	34	156	278
ORDINARY TIME			
Proper 1	36	158	280
Proper 2	38	160	282
Proper 3	40	162	284
Second Sunday before Lent	42	164	286
Sunday before Lent	44	166	288

	Year A	Year B	Year C

LENT

	Year A	Year B	Year C
First Sunday of Lent	46	168	290
Second Sunday of Lent	48	170	292
Third Sunday of Lent	50	172	294
Fourth Sunday of Lent: Mothering Sunday	52	174	296
Fifth Sunday of Lent	54	176	298
Palm Sunday	56	178	300

EASTER

	Year A	Year B	Year C
Easter Day	58	180	302
Second Sunday of Easter	60	182	304
Third Sunday of Easter	62	184	306
Fourth Sunday of Easter	64	186	308
Fifth Sunday of Easter	66	188	310
Sixth Sunday of Easter	68	190	312
Ascension Day	70	192	314
Seventh Sunday of Easter	72	194	316
Pentecost	74	196	318

ORDINARY TIME

	Year A	Year B	Year C
Trinity Sunday	76	198	320
Proper 4	78	200	322
Proper 5	80	202	324
Proper 6	82	204	326
Proper 7	84	206	328
Proper 8	86	208	330
Proper 9	88	210	332
Proper 10	90	212	334
Proper 11	92	214	336
Proper 12	94	216	338
Proper 13	96	218	340
Proper 14	98	220	342

	Year A	Year B	Year C
Proper 15	100	222	344
Proper 16	102	224	346
Proper 17	104	226	348
Proper 18	106	228	350
Proper 19	108	230	352
Proper 20	110	232	354
Proper 21	112	234	356
Proper 22	114	236	358
Proper 23	116	238	360
Proper 24	118	240	362
Proper 25	120	242	364
All Saints' Day	122	244	366
Fourth Sunday before Advent	124	246	368
Third Sunday before Advent	126	248	370
Second Sunday before Advent	128	250	372
Christ the King	130	252	374

Year A

FIRST SUNDAY OF ADVENT

*We are to wake up and make sure
we stay ready for the second coming.*

Let us pray to the God of all time and space,
in whose love we exist
and by whose love we are saved.

As we prepare ourselves
for the time when Christ comes again in glory,
we pray for the grace and honesty
to see what needs transforming in our lives as individuals
and as members of the Church of God.

Silence

O come:
let us walk in the light of the Lord.

May all church leaders, pastors and teachers be directed,
inspired and upheld by the living Spirit of God,
and may there be a deepening
of love and commitment in all Christians the world over.

Silence

O come:
let us walk in the light of the Lord.

May the leaders of this nation and of all the nations
be drawn increasingly to understand
God's ways of justice and righteousness,
and be filled with the longing
to do what is right and honest and good.

Silence

O come:
let us walk in the light of the Lord.

May all the families on earth be blessed with mutual love
and caring consideration one of another;
may arguments and misunderstandings
be properly resolved,
and difficult relationships refreshed and healed.

Silence

O come:
let us walk in the light of the Lord.

May those for whom the days and nights
creep past in pain or sorrow be given comfort and hope;
may the frightened find reassurance
and the anxious find peace of mind.

Silence

O come:
let us walk in the light of the Lord.

May those who have reached the point of death
be given the knowledge of God's closeness
on that last journey;
and may those who have died
know the eternal peace and joy of heaven.

Silence

O come:
let us walk in the light of the Lord.

May we all be given a new enthusiasm
for walking God's way, clothed in the armour of light.

Merciful Father,
accept these prayers
for the sake of your Son,
our Saviour Jesus Christ. Amen.

SECOND SUNDAY OF ADVENT

Get the road ready for the Lord!

Our God is always ready to hear our prayers.
Let us be still, and pray to him now.

Heavenly Father,
we thank you for all those who remind us
to be kind and loving by their words and example.
We pray that as a church
we may get ready to welcome you
and put right whatever blocks us from your love.

Silence

Come to us, Lord:
we know our need of you.

We pray that the lines of communication
between people and nations
may be kept open, respected and honoured,
and that where communication has broken down
there may be a new desire for healing.

Silence

Come to us, Lord:
we know our need of you.

Heavenly Father,
we pray for all those making and repairing roads,
travelling on them and stuck in traffic jams;
we pray for the towns and villages linked by roads,
for a public transport system that protects the environment,
and serves the community.

Silence

Come to us, Lord:
we know our need of you.

We pray for those we see and talk to
every day or every week;
for those we often argue with or misunderstand;
for those who brighten our lives and make us smile;
for a greater thankfulness and appreciation
of those we usually take for granted.

Silence

Come to us, Lord:
we know our need of you.

We pray for those we have hurt or upset;
for those who feel isolated and alone;
for the ill, the frail, the stressed and the bitter.

Silence

Come to us, Lord:
we know our need of you.

We pray for the dying
and those who have died to this earthly life.
May they know the eternal peace of your heaven,
and may those who miss them be comforted.

Silence

Come to us, Lord:
we know our need of you.

Heavenly Father, we thank you for helping us
to get ourselves ready to receive you.

Merciful Father,
**accept these prayers
for the sake of your Son,
our Saviour Jesus Christ. Amen.**

THIRD SUNDAY OF ADVENT

Great expectations.
Jesus fulfils the great statements of prophecy.

Knowing that our God loves us and listens,
let us pray to him now.

Lord, your Church is so full of possibility
and yet so vulnerable;
it is so urgently needed by our world and yet often so weak;
strengthen each member of the body
and increase our sense of expectation
so that we live with your life.

Silence

Faithful God:
you are the rock we stand on.

Lord, in our constantly changing world,
with its shifting values and fragile ecological balance,
root us deeply in your unchanging nature
of mercy, goodness, faithfulness and love.

Silence

Faithful God:
you are the rock we stand on.

Lord, we welcome you into our homes,
our streets, and our communities;
where we are blind to your presence, give us sight;
in the ordinary and the remarkable,
help us to recognise our true and living God.

Silence

Faithful God:
you are the rock we stand on.

Lord, all the needs of your children
are known to you;
with God-given love we bring to mind
those who are suffering physically,
spiritually or emotionally,
that they may find you there beside them
in these dark and painful times.

Silence

Faithful God:
you are the rock we stand on.

Lord, to whom eternity is natural,
help us to realise that time is not the whole story,
and welcome into your kingdom
those who have lived this life in your company
and have now passed through death;
comfort those of us here
whose hearts are heavy with grieving.

Silence

Faithful God:
you are the rock we stand on.

Lord, awaken us to expect you with joy;
we give you thanks for your tender parenting
and your unfailing patience with us.

Merciful Father,
**accept these our prayers
for the sake of your Son,
our Saviour Jesus Christ. Amen.**

FOURTH SUNDAY OF ADVENT

Through the willing participation of Mary and Joseph,
God is poised to come among his people as their Saviour.

Let us quieten ourselves to notice our God,
here with us now,
and attentive to our deepest needs.

Lord, we long for our Church to be alive and active,
attentive to you,
and ready to go wherever you suggest.
Show us the work of the Church
from your point of view,
and develop our will to co-operate.

Silence

We call on your name, O God:
restore us and revive us.

Lord, we long for your kingdom
to come in our world,
and to flood with truth and love
the disillusion, hopelessness and terror
which traps the human spirit
and chokes its potential joy.

Silence

We call on your name, O God:
restore us and revive us.

Lord, come into the daily relationships
we so easily take for granted,
and enable us to value one another,
delighting in one another's richness,
and responding to one another's needs with love.

Silence

We call on your name, O God:
restore us and revive us.

Lord, you know the need and pain
of those we love and worry about.
As you look after them,
give them the sense of your caring presence
to uphold and sustain them.

Silence

We call on your name, O God:
restore us and revive us.

Lord, for us death can seem so cruel;
give us a better understanding of eternity,
and gather into your kingdom all those
whose earthly journey has come to an end.

Silence

We call on your name, O God:
restore us and revive us.

Thank you, Lord of hope,
for the way you surprise us with joy,
and show us the extraordinary and the wonderful
in the ordinary things of life.

Merciful Father,
accept these prayers
for the sake of your Son,
our Saviour Jesus Christ. Amen.

CHRISTMAS DAY

*The Word of God is made flesh. In the birth of Jesus
we see God expressed in human terms.*

As we celebrate the birth of Jesus, the Word of God,
let us pray with thankful hearts.

The bells and lights and presents and decorations
in church and in our homes
express our thanks to you, Lord,
for coming into the world in person.

Silence

On this Christmas Day we want to say:
Thank you, holy God!

The world Jesus was born into was the world we know.
Thank you for being prepared to face the dangers and risks
of human mistakes and sin in order to save us.

Silence

On this Christmas Day we want to say:
Thank you, holy God!

Many of us will be celebrating
with our families and friends.
We invite you to join us in all the festivities,
and ask you to teach us true loving.

Silence

On this Christmas Day we want to say:
Thank you, holy God!

We remember those who find Christmas
a sad or lonely season;
we remember those for whom it brings to the surface
memories, anxieties or dangers.
Through good and difficult times
you are always with us.

Silence

On this Christmas Day we want to say:
Thank you, holy God!

We remember those
whose loved ones have died,
and all those who have finished
with earthly celebrations.
May they celebrate with you
and all the angels of heaven.

Silence

On this Christmas Day we want to say:
Thank you, holy God!

For all the many blessings of this past year
and for all the good that you have enabled us to do;
for the experiences that have taught us
humility and patience,
we thank you.

Silence

On this Christmas Day we want to say:
Thank you, holy God!

Merciful Father,
accept these prayers
for the sake of your Son,
our Saviour Jesus Christ. Amen.

FIRST SUNDAY OF CHRISTMAS

*Jesus, the expression of God's love, lives as a vulnerable
boy in the real and dangerous world we all inhabit.*

Let us pray to the God who travels with us
in all our celebrations and tragedies,
and understands what it is like to be human.

As we celebrate Christmas,
when the Word of God became flesh,
we pray for the Church, the Body of Christ.
May we be so filled with God's loving life
that our actions touch the world with hope
which lasts even when Christmas decorations
are put away.

Silence

Thank you, Lord God:
for coming to save us.

As the world is reminded of love and peace
in the words of the carols,
may the reality of a God who loves us so much
transform our social and political thinking,
and energise our plans and negotiations.

Silence

Thank you, Lord God:
for coming to save us.

As Christmas brings together family members and friends,
and we make contact with those we seldom meet,
may all our relationships be nourished
with love and forgiveness,
and may we value one another more.

Silence

Thank you, Lord God:
for coming to save us.

We remember all who are forced to escape
from their homes, and live without security;
we think particularly of those with young children
who are homeless or in danger.

Silence

Thank you, Lord God:
for coming to save us.

We pray for those whose earthly journey
has come to an end,
and those who have tended them during their dying;
we pray for those who have died through violence,
and for those who have much to forgive.

Silence

Thank you, Lord God:
for coming to save us.

Lord, we recognise our great need of your grace,
and give you thanks and praise
for making possible what would otherwise
be impossible.

Merciful Father,
accept these prayers
for the sake of your Son,
our Saviour Jesus Christ. Amen.

SECOND SUNDAY OF CHRISTMAS

*The grace and truth revealed in Jesus show God's
freely-given love; through Jesus, God pours out his
blessings on us and gives us real freedom.*

Let us settle ourselves in the stillness of God's peace
as we pray.

Lord, may the Church clear away any barriers
which prevent your love from flooding it.
Wash away all but what is constructed out of your love
and built on your foundations.

Silence

O come:
let us adore.

Lord, may our world become sensitised
to hear the whispered voice of your love;
may we honour your creation
and value one another as you value us.

Silence

O come:
let us adore.

Lord, may we receive you into our homes and families,
our shops, schools and places of work;
may we receive you into our conflicts,
our arguments and our expectations.

Silence

O come:
let us adore.

Lord, even as we thank you for giving us free will,
we pray for those suffering
as a tragic result of wrong choices.
May they experience your upholding and healing
in body and soul.

Silence

O come:
let us adore.

Lord, may those who are journeying
through death to eternity,
be awakened to the everlasting love
of your Presence.

Silence

O come:
let us adore.

Lord, to whom else could we go?
You alone have the words of eternal life!

Merciful Father,
**accept these prayers
for the sake of your Son,
our Saviour Jesus Christ. Amen.**

THE EPIPHANY

Jesus, the hope of the nations, is shown to the world.

We are all companions on a spiritual journey.
As we travel together, let us pray.

Silence

Light of the world:
shine in our darkness.

We pray that the worldwide Church
may always be ready
to travel in your way
and in your direction.

Silence

Light of the world:
shine in our darkness.

We pray for the nations
as they live through conflicts
and struggle with identity.
We long for all peoples
to acknowledge the true and living God.

Silence

Light of the world:
shine in our darkness.

We pray for the families and the streets we represent,
asking for a spirit of generous love,
understanding and mutual respect.

Silence

Light of the world:
shine in our darkness.

We pray for all who are finding their way
tedious, lonely or frightening at the moment;
for those who have lost their way
and do not know what to do for the best.

Silence

Light of the world:
shine in our darkness.

We pray for those who have come
to the end of their earthly journey,
and for those who have died unprepared.

Silence

Light of the world:
shine in our darkness.

We offer our thanks and praise
for the way you see us when we are still far off
and welcome us home.

Merciful Father,
**accept these prayers
for the sake of your Son,
our Saviour Jesus Christ. Amen.**

THE BAPTISM OF CHRIST
FIRST SUNDAY OF EPIPHANY

As Jesus is baptised, the Spirit of God rests visibly on him,
marking him out as the One who will save his people.

Let us attune our hearts to the God who loves us.

God of love,
we pray for all those who are newly baptised,
or who have recently found that you are real;
we pray for all in ordained and lay ministries,
and for those sensing a special calling.
Help us all to listen to your guiding.

Silence

In God:
all things work together for good.

God of power,
we pray for those who are in authority
and in positions of influence and responsibility;
may they be earthed in humility, courageous in integrity,
and mindful of the need to serve.

Silence

In God:
all things work together for good.

God of mercy,
we call to mind those with whom we share
the work and leisure of our life;
we pray for those we treasure and those we battle with,
and ask you to breathe into all our relationships
the forgiving love which cleanses and heals.

Silence

In God:
all things work together for good.

God of wholeness,
we remember those who are aching today
in body, mind or spirit;
knowing that nothing is unredeemable,
we ask that you will bring good
even out of these barren places.

Silence

In God:
all things work together for good.

God of life,
we pray for those whose earthly lives have ended;
we remember those who have died
violently and tragically, suddenly and unprepared.
We give you thanks for lives well lived
and for happy memories.
May they rest in the eternal peace of heaven.

Silence

In God:
all things work together for good.

God of faithfulness,
we thank you for the way
you always keep your promises
and never let us down.

Merciful Father,
accept these prayers
for the sake of your Son,
our Saviour Jesus Christ. Amen.

SECOND SUNDAY OF EPIPHANY

*Jesus is recognised and pointed out by John
to be God's chosen one.*

Let us voice our cares and concerns,
knowing that God is listening to us.

Lord God, make yourself known
to the people who come into our churches,
or who pass by and sometimes wonder,
but have not yet come in;
make us better bearers of your life
to those who need you but have never met you.

Silence

True and living God:
we want to know you more.

Lord God, the world lurches from crisis to crisis,
and there is much misleading and misdirecting;
help us recover the natural sense
of what is right and just, honest and good,
so that our hearts are inclined
to hear the voice of your leading and respond to it.

Silence

True and living God:
we want to know you more.

Lord God, help us to take more seriously
our responsibility of helping one another
forward into faith, as brothers and sisters;
we pray for those in our own families
whom we would love to bring to know you,
and for those who have drifted away.

Silence

True and living God:
we want to know you more.

Lord God, there are some who are going through
very distressing, painful and worrying times.
We stand alongside them now,
and ask for them your comfort, reassurance,
healing and peace of mind.

Silence

True and living God:
we want to know you more.

Lord God, even as we pray now,
there are those journeying through death.
We pray for them, for all who have recently died,
and for all those left without their loved ones,
grieving, or numbed with shock.

Silence

True and living God:
we want to know you more.

Lord God, we thank you for all those
who have directed us to know you better,
and for the way you are drawing us closer
into friendship with you.

Merciful Father,
accept these prayers
for the sake of your Son,
our Saviour Jesus Christ. Amen.

THIRD SUNDAY OF EPIPHANY

*The prophecies of Isaiah are fulfilled in a new
and lasting way in Jesus of Nazareth.*

Let us pray to the loving God we have seen in Jesus.

We pray that the light of God
will shine in all the dark corners of the Church,
and set us free from prejudice,
small-mindedness and hypocrisy;
that as members of the Body of Christ
we can move freely through the power of God
wherever we are called to go,
available and active in God's service.

Silence

Lord God of power:
set us free to live.

We pray that our world may be lit
by this light in the darkness
to bring freedom and hope wherever there is oppression,
recognition and respect where there is none,
and in all conflicts positive ways forward.

Silence

Lord God of power:
set us free to live.

We pray that in our homes, our workplaces
and our neighbourhoods
the light of godly loving may soften harsh edges,
encourage mutual caring,
and heal dysfunctional or damaging relationships.

Silence

Lord God of power:
set us free to live.

We pray that all those whose lives
are fettered by the past,
by rejection, guilt, pain or anxiety,
may be set free and encouraged to live to the full.

Silence

Lord God of power:
set us free to live.

We pray for those who have died,
and those who miss them
and are finding it very hard to cope with their loss.
We pray for all those who have no one to help them
through that last journey.

Silence

Lord God of power:
set us free to live.

Thank you, Father,
for transforming our suffering and our mistakes
again and again and again.

Merciful Father,
accept these prayers
for the sake of your Son,
our Saviour Jesus Christ. Amen.

FOURTH SUNDAY OF EPIPHANY

Jesus shows us in action the loving
provision of the God who made us.

Let us pray to the God of love,
who listens to the people of his making.

Holy God, we bring before you all that we are,
with as much honesty and openness as we can.
We know your Church is weakened
by disunity, misplaced priorities, complacency and fear.
We pray for a new awakening of our calling
to be the people of God;
give us a fresh understanding of your will
and empower us with nothing short of your life
lived out in us.

Silence

You alone are our God:
and we trust in you.

Holy God, give all the nations and peoples of our world
such respect and love for creation
that we learn to take proper responsibility
for the resources we share and the universe we inhabit.
Give us courage to make good decisions
even if they involve us in conflict or discomfort.

Silence

You alone are our God:
and we trust in you.

Holy God, we pray for a greater awareness
of your presence in our homes and places of work,
in our cars and in public transport,
in the shops, schools and hospitals,

and wherever people meet together.
Teach us how to live lovingly,
with honesty and compassion;
teach us how to live thankfully,
and work on our habit of grumbling.

Silence

You alone are our God:
and we trust in you.

Holy God, we bring to you those we know
who are suffering with prolonged illness,
debilitating pain, and emotional distress.
Lay your hands on them to bring relief and healing,
courage to live through this dark time,
and the inner strength which only you can give.

Silence

You alone are our God:
and we trust in you.

Holy God, we pray for those
making the journey through death,
and for those who have died to this earthly life.
Thank you for all they have given us.
Comfort those who miss them,
and through your mercy receive us all, in our time,
to live in the peace and joy of your eternity.

Silence

You alone are our God:
and we trust in you.

Holy God, we thank you for making yourself known to us
in the many blessings of life,
and most of all in the person of Jesus, the Christ.

Merciful Father,
**accept these prayers
for the sake of your Son,
our Saviour Jesus Christ. Amen.**

PROPER 1

Sunday between 3 and 9 February inclusive
(if earlier than the Second Sunday before Lent)

*We are commissioned to live so that we shine like lights
which direct others on to God, the source of Light.*

Let us pray to the God who has drawn us here today,
who loves us, and loves our world.

We pray that there may be a revival of longing
for your kingdom to come,
and a renewed commitment to working for it;
for a desire to live out our faith and worship
in our daily lives this week.

Silence

Come, Holy Spirit:
set our hearts on fire.

We pray that all who have authority and power
in our nation and our world may use it for good,
upholding and instigating what is right and fair,
and listening to the needs of those they represent.
May we recognise our responsibility
to support and stand up for God's values.

Silence

Come, Holy Spirit:
set our hearts on fire.

We pray that within our homes and communities
there may be a new awareness
of one another's gifts and needs,
more sensitivity and respect in our relationships;
may we reverence one another as fellow beings,
born of your creative love.

Silence

Come, Holy Spirit:
set our hearts on fire.

We pray for all who are oppressed,
downtrodden or despised;
we pray for those who will not eat today
and all who live in the degrading circumstances
of poverty and powerlessness;
we pray for a heart to put injustices right
and strive for a fair sharing of resources.

Silence

Come, Holy Spirit:
set our hearts on fire.

We pray for those whose life expectancy is short,
for the babies and children who have died
while we have been praying;
for all who have come to the end of their earthly life
and made that last journey through death;
thank you for your welcoming mercy
and the promise of eternal life.

Silence

Come, Holy Spirit:
set our hearts on fire.

We offer you our thanks and praise
for the scriptures that remind and inspire us,
and for your living Spirit which enables us.

Merciful Father,
**accept these prayers
for the sake of your Son,
our Saviour Jesus Christ. Amen.**

PROPER 2

Sunday between 10 and 16 February inclusive
(if earlier than the Second Sunday before Lent)

To live God's way is to choose the way of life.

Gathered together in one spirit, let us pray to our God.

Father, wherever our attention
has wandered from your calling,
wherever we have fallen short of your will for us,
and failed to keep the spirit of your law of love,
forgive us and transform us,
so that we walk again the path that leads to life.

Silence

Show us the way of life:
and help us to walk in it.

Wherever the Church is asked
to give leadership on sensitive issues;
whenever the current world expectations of behaviour
need to be challenged in the light of God's love,
give us the wisdom and guidance we need.

Silence

Show us the way of life:
and help us to walk in it.

Wherever our homes are lacking
in love and mutual respect,
wherever destructive relationships
cause distress and heartache,
and wherever people are made to feel they don't matter,
give a new realisation of your ways
and your hopes for us, so that your kingdom may come
and your will be done.

Silence

Show us the way of life:
and help us to walk in it.

Wherever there is illness, unhappiness, injustice or fear;
wherever people feel frustrated, imprisoned or trapped;
give us a greater sense of loving community,
a heart to put right whatever we can,
and the willingness to stand
alongside one another in our sorrows.

Silence

Show us the way of life:
and help us to walk in it.

Wherever earthly lives have come to an end,
and people are grieving the loss of their loved ones,
fill these places with the eternal peace of your presence
and prepare us all through our lives on this earth
for everlasting life with you in heaven.

Silence

Show us the way of life:
and help us to walk in it.

Father, we thank you
for the personal and affectionate way you care for us
and provide for all our needs;
may we spread the good news of your love
by the way we respond to you and to one another.

Merciful Father,
**accept these prayers
for the sake of your Son,
our Saviour Jesus Christ. Amen.**

PROPER 3

Sunday between 17 and 23 February inclusive
(if earlier than the Second Sunday before Lent)

We are called to be holy; to be perfect in our generous loving,
because that is what God our Father is like.

God has chosen to call us here and we have chosen to come.
Let us pray to him now.

Lord, we want to pray for stronger faith
and the courage to live up to our calling;
for the grace to act always
with the generosity of spirit you show to us,
until the whole Church models the wisdom
which the world counts as foolishness.

Silence

Holy God:
we commit ourselves to your service.

Lord, we want to pray
about all the unresolved conflicts in our world.
We ask you to give us your desire for peace,
your spirit of discernment,
your understanding of unspoken needs,
and your capacity for forgiveness.

Silence

Holy God:
we commit ourselves to your service.

Lord, we want to pray
for the homes and families we represent,
and for all with whom we live and work.
Help us to recognise the opportunities
for generous, loving service
and take away any destructive possessiveness
or self-interest.

Silence

Holy God:
we commit ourselves to your service.

Lord, we pray for peace of mind and spirit
in all those who are distressed or enveloped in pain.
May they know the reality of your inner healing,
and may even the worst situations
become places of growth and new life.

Silence

Holy God:
we commit ourselves to your service.

Lord, we pray for those approaching death
with fear, resentment and anger,
and for all who counsel the dying and the bereaved.
We pray that those who have died will know
the joy of everlasting life with you.

Silence

Holy God:
we commit ourselves to your service.

Lord, we thank you
for the extraordinary generosity of your love,
which takes us by surprise and refreshes us,
and which always appears
where we least think to look for it.

Merciful Father,
accept these prayers
for the sake of your Son,
our Saviour Jesus Christ. Amen.

SECOND SUNDAY BEFORE LENT

God is creative and good; seeking his rule, as our priority,
will mean that everything else falls into place.

Let us pray to the God who knows us so well
and understands our needs.

Lord, in all the daily concerns of parish life,
and in the great issues facing the whole Church,
may we never lose sight of your priorities
but see everything through the eyes of compassion,
with honesty and integrity.

Silence

Lord of creation:
let your kingdom come!

Lord, in the local issues of this community,
and in the difficulties and dilemmas on the world stage,
may we look for the face of Christ
and fix our attention on his underlying values
of love, justice and mercy.

Silence

Lord of creation:
let your kingdom come!

Lord, in all the minor squabbles
and major rifts of family life,
may we know the assurance of your promise
to be with us always,
and your power to transform and renew.

Silence

Lord of creation:
let your kingdom come!

Lord, in the shock of sudden illness and pain,
and in the wearing endurance of long-term weakness,
give your peace and tranquillity,
your healing and hope.

Silence

Lord of creation:
let your kingdom come!

Lord, through the journey of death
and in the grieving of those who mourn,
gather us up into the everlasting arms of love
and comfort us,
and bring us to life in all its fullness.

Silence

Lord of creation:
let your kingdom come!

Lord, we thank you
that we can trust you completely
and you never let us down!

Merciful Father,
accept these prayers
for the sake of your Son,
our Saviour Jesus Christ. Amen.

SUNDAY BEFORE LENT

In Jesus the full glory of God is revealed and encountered.

As children together in the family of God,
let us pray now to our Father in heaven.

Lord, we pray that as Christians
we may listen more attentively
and with greater urgency than ever before
to the words of Jesus;
give us more awareness of your presence with us,
both in our worship and in our daily ministry,
giving us the courage to live out your truth with joy.

Silence

Holy God:
transform us and use us to your glory.

We pray for those who do not know you
or dismiss you as irrelevant to their lives;
we pray for those who influence and encourage others
in what is evil, destructive or depraved,
and ask for your protection
of all who are vulnerable and in danger.

Silence

Holy God:
transform us and use us to your glory.

We pray for all who are adjusting
to new relationships in the family,
new homes or new work and leisure patterns;
we pray for stronger root growth in you,
so that we are not thrown
by the changes and troubles of everyday life,
knowing the reality of your faithfulness.

Silence

Holy God:
transform us and use us to your glory.

We pray for all who are too exhausted
or overwhelmed by circumstances and pressures
to be able to pray;
surround all those who are troubled
and heavily laden
with the revitalising assurance of your presence,
your understanding and your love.

Silence

Holy God:
transform us and use us to your glory.

We pray that those who have gone through death
may know the brightness of everlasting life
in your company;
may we, with them, come to experience
the glory and joy of heaven.

Silence

Holy God:
transform us and use us to your glory.

Father, we thank you for the glimpses of glory
you give us in this life, for your friendship
and your promise to be with us always.

Merciful Father,
accept these prayers
for the sake of your Son,
our Saviour Jesus Christ. Amen.

FIRST SUNDAY
OF LENT

Jesus knows all about temptation;
and he can deal with our sin.

Our God knows us and the temptations we face.
Let us pray to him now.

As the Church begins this season of Lent
we ask you to remind us of what is important
and what is not;
of where we are wandering away
and what we need to change;
so that by Easter
we will be renewed and strengthened
for your service in the world.

Silence

The Lord is God:
there is no other.

The world's misery and pain
and desperate need of healing
are clear to see and affect us all.
We pray now for this damaged world
with all its weakness, longings and failings,
with all its potential and hope.

Silence

The Lord is God:
there is no other.

Whenever a child is born
we celebrate the creative hope of God.
We pray for all being born this week
and for their families and communities,
that all our children may be loved and cared for,
safe and happy.

Silence

The Lord is God:
there is no other.

We pray for all who suffer through others' sin;
all victims of abuse or oppression or apathy;
all whose adult lives are distorted and misshapen
by early damaging experiences
which need your healing.

Silence

The Lord is God:
there is no other.

We remember those who,
freed from the ageing and pain of their bodies,
can live now with you
in the peace and joy of heaven.

Silence

The Lord is God:
there is no other.

Lord, we give you thanks and praise
for the hope we have in Jesus;
for the strength to resist temptation
and the joy and relief of forgiveness when we fall.

Merciful Father,
accept these prayers
for the sake of your Son,
our Saviour Jesus Christ. Amen.

SECOND SUNDAY OF LENT

*Anyone who believes in Jesus can know
his power to save and set us free.*

Loving God, because we trust you,
we come to you now with our concerns
for the Church and the world.

We bring all those who find it so hard to believe,
so hard to trust in a faithful loving God;
we bring those who teach the faith;
all who preach and chat the good news.
Give the right words for each situation and each person,
and enable the seed to take root and grow.

Silence

In you, O Lord:
we put our trust.

We bring those whose authority and decisions
affect the lives of many people and the health of the planet.
We pray for sensitivity and honesty,
and the strength to retain integrity
even in positions of power.

Silence

In you, O Lord:
we put our trust.

We bring the newly born and their parents,
and all whose family circumstances face change;
give us the spiritual flexibility
to adapt to your guiding in all our relationships,
and above all in our relationship with you.

Silence

In you, O Lord:
we put our trust.

We bring all for whom illness or injury
has caused disruption, uncertainty
and the prospect of long-term change;
all who find their lives are spinning
out of their control;
give them working knowledge
of your total loving and unchanging presence,
so that in all the changes and troubles of life
they may be assured of your everlasting protection.

Silence

In you, O Lord:
we put our trust.

We commend to your love and mercy
all those who have made the journey through death,
especially any who have died unprepared,
or violent deaths.
We thank you for your understanding and compassion
and pray that they may know the forgiveness,
peace and joy of heaven.

Silence

In you, O Lord:
we put our trust.

As we call to mind the guidance and help
you give us each moment of every day,
we thank you and praise you, Holy God,
for you alone have the words of eternal life.

Merciful Father,
**accept these prayers
for the sake of your Son,
our Saviour Jesus Christ. Amen.**

THIRD SUNDAY OF LENT

*God both knows us completely and loves us
completely; meeting us where we are, he provides us
with living water, to satisfy all our needs.*

Thirsty for God, let us pray to him now,
in the knowledge that he will provide for us
in the way that is best.

Father, wherever the Church is dry and parched
may the water of your Spirit well up to refresh and renew,
to bring life and strong new growth.
Lord, make us more aware of our thirst for you,
so that we come to you ready and eager
to receive your living water.

Silence

Living God:
satisfy our thirst.

Father, from the conflicting needs
and agendas of the world we cry for mercy,
for a deeper understanding of one another
and a greater desire for co-operation and peace.
We pray for sensitivity in handling delicate negotiations
and the wisdom which respects and listens.

Silence

Living God:
satisfy our thirst.

We pray that in all our relationships
you will make us effective channels
of your love and forgiveness.
Make us awash with your living water
so that our homes and places of work,

our shopping and leisure centres,
our conversations and actions,
are always in touch with the renewing power of God.

Silence

Living God:
satisfy our thirst.

We stand alongside all those who are suffering,
whether in body, mind or spirit,
and long for your healing and comfort,
your strength for perseverance
and your patience in the dark times;
we long for your living Spirit to envelop and sustain them.

Silence

Living God:
satisfy our thirst.

We pray for those who have come
to the end of earthly life; have mercy on them.
May they, placing their faith in the God of life,
share in the light and joy of heaven for ever.

Silence

Living God:
satisfy our thirst.

O God, how we need you!
We thank you for supplying us and coaxing us forward
with such tenderness and affection.

Merciful Father,
**accept these prayers
for the sake of your Son,
our Saviour Jesus Christ. Amen.**

FOURTH SUNDAY OF LENT
MOTHERING SUNDAY

*Thanking God for our earthly opportunities for
mothering and being mothered, we also remember
the mothering parenthood of God.*

Let us pray to our loving parent God,
as children in one family.

We thank you, loving God,
for giving us one another to enjoy,
to laugh and cry with, to learn to live with.
May even our conflicts and arguments be used
in helping us to grow up in your love.

Silence

Loving God:
we give you thanks.

Thank you, loving God, for showing us the way to love
and giving us opportunities to give,
to take second place, to accept people as they are,
to forgive them when they annoy us,
and look for their needs before our own.

Silence

Loving God:
we give you thanks.

Thank you, loving God, for the world we live in,
for the colours and shapes, the sounds and textures in it.
Thank you for giving us minds and emotions
and help us to reverence the whole of creation.

Silence

Loving God:
we give you thanks.

Thank you, loving God, for comfort and sympathy,
reassurance and practical caring when we are ill or sad.
Make us all more aware of the needs of those around us
and let our loving show in action.

Silence

Loving God:
we give you thanks.

Thank you, loving God,
for your promise to be with us always,
and not just until we die.
We remember with affection
those of our parents who loved us into existence
and now live in eternity.
Gather up into your loving arms
those who have recently died
and comfort all whose memories
make them aware of loss today.

Silence

Loving God:
we give you thanks.

Thank you, loving God, for giving us space and support,
guidance and forgiveness, challenge and reassurance.

Merciful Father,
**accept these prayers
for the sake of your Son,
our Saviour Jesus Christ. Amen.**

FIFTH SUNDAY
OF LENT

*Jesus is the resurrection and the life. He can transform
death and despair, in any form, into life and hope.*

As the people of the living God,
let us join together in our prayers
for the Church and for the world.

Holy God, breathe your life into the Church;
breathe holiness and deepening faith,
breathe energy, inspired teaching and fervent praise;
unblock the channels and make us more receptive
to your gentleness and your power.

Silence

Breathe into us:
so that we live in you.

Holy God, breathe your life into the universe;
breathe responsible caring, honesty and compassion,
breathe right values and good stewardship,
peace and reconciliation, vision and hope.

Silence

Breathe into us:
so that we live in you.

Holy God, breathe your life
into our homes and places of work;
breathe increased patience and understanding,
and the courage to live the Christian life
when to do so brings ridicule or demands sacrifice.

Silence

Breathe into us:
so that we live in you.

Holy God, breathe your life into those who suffer;
breathe comfort and wholeness,
forgiveness and new confidence,
breathe peace of mind
and the knowledge of your love.

Silence

Breathe into us:
so that we live in you.

Holy God, breathe your life into the dead and dying;
breathe courage for the journey
and the realisation that you can be trusted.
Breathe life that lasts for ever.

Silence

Breathe into us:
so that we live in you.

Holy God, breathe your life into us now
as we offer you here our thanks and praise
for your life laid down out of love for us.
May our words be worked out
in fresh commitment to you.

Merciful Father,
**accept these prayers
for the sake of your Son,
our Saviour Jesus Christ. Amen.**

PALM SUNDAY

Jesus rides into Jerusalem cheered by the crowds.
Days later crowds will be clamouring for his death.

As we recall the extent of God's love for us,
let us pray.

Father, if we as the Church
are truly to be the body of Christ,
then let us stand at the foot of the cross
and learn what it means to love and keep on loving;
to serve and keep on serving.

Silence

God our Father:
let your will be done in us.

If the world is ever to see real hope,
then purify and transform our lives
and stretch out our arms in loving forgiveness,
with no exceptions and no small print,
so that we shine as lights in the darkness.

Silence

God our Father:
let your will be done in us.

If our work places and neighbourhoods and homes
are to display and respond to your values,
then make us more fervent in prayer,
more courageous in self-discipline
and, above all, more loving in outreach.

Silence

God our Father:
let your will be done in us.

If the terrible suffering of extreme poverty,
injustice and oppression is to be addressed realistically,
then take away our greed and complacency
and our assumptions about appropriate living standards,
and teach us sacrificial self-giving
of time, energy and resources.

Silence

God our Father:
let your will be done in us.

Father, through the life-giving death of Jesus,
may the dying turn to you
and know your merciful love;
may the grieving be comforted,
and may we all one day share
with those who have died
the eternal joy of your heaven.

Silence

God our Father:
let your will be done in us.

Father, such amazing love is hard to grasp
and impossible to repay.
In thankfulness for lives set free to live
we offer you ourselves.

Merciful Father,
accept these prayers
for the sake of your Son,
our Saviour Jesus Christ. Amen.

EASTER DAY

It is true. Jesus is alive for all time. The Lord of life
cannot be held by death. God's victory over sin and
death means that new life for us is a reality.

As we celebrate the new life of Resurrection,
let us pray to the one true God, who brings us all to life.

Lord God, we pray that the Church
may proclaim with joy your message of hope
for the world;
may our lives, as well as our worship,
testify to the truth of the Resurrection;
broaden our vision of what is possible
through new life in you.

Silence

Life-giving God:
transform our lives.

Lord God, we pray for the world we inhabit;
for those who lead, and take important decisions,
and for those who follow or are coerced,
or who have no voice.
We pray for mercy and justice, compassion and integrity.
We pray for protection against evil
and strengthening of goodness.

Silence

Life-giving God:
transform our lives.

Lord God, we pray for all babies, and those as yet unborn,
that they may be born into a world of love and acceptance.
We pray, too, for those who provide foster care,
and for all children at risk.
We pray for all parents and those who support them.

We pray for the newly baptised and recently confirmed;
for a deeper commitment to supporting one another
as we grow in faith.

Silence

Life-giving God:
transform our lives.

Lord God, we pray for those who cannot think,
for the pain or anguish which engulfs them;
for all whose lives are troubled and insecure;
for those who have little energy left to rejoice.
Bring healing, and the resources to cope with suffering,
and give us the grace
to carry one another's burdens in love.

Silence

Life-giving God:
transform our lives.

Lord God, we thank you for lives well lived,
and commend to your keeping those who have died.
Through the resurrection hope,
may they know the joy of heaven.

Silence

Life-giving God:
transform our lives.

Lord God, we thank you for the precious gift of new life;
may we never again take it for granted,
but live each moment in the fullness of life
that Jesus has gained for us.

Merciful Father,
**accept these prayers
for the sake of your Son,
our Saviour Jesus Christ. Amen.**

SECOND SUNDAY OF EASTER

Through the risen Jesus we have a living hope
which will never spoil or fade.

As we gather here with God's presence in the midst of us,
let us pray.

We bring to you, Lord,
the Church in all its richness and all its need;
all its diversity and all its division.
Give us a fresh understanding
of what it means to live in you;
may all of us – both laity and clergy together –
celebrate the reality of your presence among us,
filling us with new life and new hope.

Silence

Lord in your presence:
we lift our hearts to you.

We bring to you, Lord,
our nation, our world, our universe;
all the areas that are fastened shut to hold you out;
all the bewildered confusion
about who we are and why we are here;
all the doubts and insecurity,
and all the searching for inner peace.

Silence

Lord in your presence:
we lift our hearts to you.

We bring to you, Lord, our homes and families,
and all the joys and sorrows of our relationships.
We bring the rooms in which we eat
and work and relax;
and invite you into them all.

Silence

Lord in your presence:
we lift our hearts to you.

We bring to you, Lord,
those whom life has damaged,
and all who find it difficult to trust in you;
we bring you those who need refreshment and hope,
comfort, healing and inner serenity.

Silence

Lord in your presence:
we lift our hearts to you.

We bring to you, Lord,
those who approach death with great fear
and those who die unprepared to meet you.
Have mercy on us all, forgive us all that is past
and gather us into your everlasting kingdom
of peace and joy.

Silence

Lord in your presence:
we lift our hearts to you.

We bring to you, Lord, the love of our hearts
as we recall the extent of your love for us
which understands our frailty
and reaches out to us where we are.

Merciful Father,
accept these prayers
for the sake of your Son,
our Saviour Jesus Christ. Amen.

THIRD SUNDAY OF EASTER

Jesus explains the scriptures and is
recognised in the breaking of bread.

As we gather to hear the word of God
and to break bread in the presence of Jesus,
let us pray.

Walk with us, Lord, on our journey of faith,
both as individuals and as the Church of God;
open up to us the truths you long for us to understand,
and inspire all who teach and encourage.
Equip us all to pass on the good news of Easter.

Silence

Lord God:
abide with us.

Walk with us, Lord, down the streets
of our cities, towns and villages,
drive with us down the motorways
and fly with us down the air corridors.
Meet all those who are curious, searching,
or moving in the wrong direction.
Let your presence be sought
and recognised in all the world.

Silence

Lord God:
abide with us.

Walk with us, Lord, in our life journeys,
guiding, teaching and correcting us,
as we learn the lessons of loving
in our homes, our work and our communities.

Silence

Lord God:
abide with us.

Walk with us, Lord,
through the times of suffering and pain,
alerting us to one another's needs
and providing for us in whatever ways are best for us.
Help us to trust you through the dark times;
breathe new life and hope
into those who are close to despair.

Silence

Lord God:
abide with us.

Walk with us, Lord, through the valley of death;
may our love and prayers support those
who walk that journey today.
Draw close to them and welcome them
into the joy of heaven.

Silence

Lord God:
abide with us.

Lord, we thank you for walking with us
wherever we travel,
We thank you that you are indeed
real and alive every step of the way!

Merciful Father,
accept these prayers
for the sake of your Son,
our Saviour Jesus Christ. Amen.

FOURTH SUNDAY OF EASTER

Jesus, the Good Shepherd, has come so that
we may have life in rich abundance.

The Lord is our shepherd,
and we are the sheep of his pasture.
Let us bring to him our cares and concerns
for the Church and for the world.

Good Shepherd of the sheep, we pray for the Church;
for all congregations, for pastors
and all who minister in word and sacrament;
we pray particularly for bishops
in their shepherding of the world Church.
We pray for clear guidance and direction
in those issues which disturb us,
asking not that you lead us the easy way
but the way that is right and good.

Silence

The Lord is my shepherd:
there is nothing I shall want.

Good Shepherd of the sheep,
we pray for the world we inhabit –
the world we have inherited
and will pass on to successive generations.
Teach us to look after it carefully and wisely,
to share its gifts more fairly,
and work together to ease its sufferings.
Turn the hearts of those who are excited by evil things
and encourage the timid to speak out
for what is wholesome and good.

Silence

The Lord is my shepherd:
there is nothing I shall want.

Good Shepherd of the sheep, we pray for our
places of work, our colleagues, friends and neighbours,
and the members of our families.
We ask not for popularity at all costs,
but the grace to do your will and be your witnesses
to what it means to live lovingly,
both when this is easy and also when it hurts.

Silence

The Lord is my shepherd:
there is nothing I shall want.

Good Shepherd of the sheep,
we pray for the weak and vulnerable,
for those who must live
depending on others for every need,
and for those who are bullied, or constantly despised.
We pray for a greater reverence, one for another,
for a greater willingness
to uphold and encourage one another;
we pray for healing and wholeness.

Silence

The Lord is my shepherd:
there is nothing I shall want.

Good Shepherd of the sheep,
we pray for those who have died;
we pray for those who ache with sorrow at their going;
we commend them all into your unfailing care
which lasts throughout this life and on into eternity.

Silence

The Lord is my shepherd:
there is nothing I shall want.

Good Shepherd of the sheep, we give you thanks
that in you we are able to live through good and ill
with abundance of life.

Merciful Father,
**accept these prayers for the sake of your Son,
our Saviour Jesus Christ. Amen.**

FIFTH SUNDAY
OF EASTER

*Jesus is the Way, the Truth and the Life, through whom
we can come into the presence of God for ever.*

As living stones,
let us pray for the building up of God's Church,
and for the world God loves.

Living God, our life is in your hands,
and we offer you all that we are,
all that our past has made us, and all that we may become.
Build us up by the power of your Spirit
into a spiritual temple
where you are glorified day after day,
in all our praise and worship,
and in our love for one another.

Silence

You are my strong rock:
my strong rock and my shelter.

Living God, our planet,
with its frenzied life on its fragile skin,
is unnervingly small and vulnerable to evil.
Sharpen our consciences to sense your direction
and protect us from all that draws us away from you.
Guide our leaders in the way of truth
and realign us all to the values which are built on you.

Silence

You are my strong rock:
my strong rock and my shelter.

Living God, may the Way which Jesus shows us
be the Way we live out our daily lives
around the table, in the daylight and the dark,
in the misunderstandings, the tensions and the rush,
in the eye contact, the conversations and the growing.

Silence

You are my strong rock:
my strong rock and my shelter.

Living God, you can use
and transform all our experiences.
We lay before you now
those who are travelling through a time
of pain or anguish, tragedy or conflict
which is hard to bear.
We stand alongside them in their suffering,
and offer it to your transforming, healing love.

Silence

You are my strong rock:
my strong rock and my shelter.

Living God, we remember those who have died
and pray for them now.
Lead them out of their pain
into the light of eternity,
and keep us all in the Way that leads us
to share that everlasting life with you.

Silence

You are my strong rock:
my strong rock and my shelter.

Living God, we thank you
for showing us the Way,
in human terms that we find easier to understand.

Merciful Father,
accept these prayers
for the sake of your Son,
our Saviour Jesus Christ. Amen.

Sixth Sunday of Easter

The Spirit of truth, given to us,
enables us to discern the living, risen Christ.

As we gather in the company of the living God,
let us pray.

Lord of life, we pray that the Church
may be alive with your risen life,
refreshed and revived by the breath of your Spirit,
purified and refined like gold and silver,
so that we truly offer the possibility
of saving love to the searching world.

Silence

You are the one true God:
and we worship you.

Lord of life, we pray that in all meetings and conferences
where important decisions are taken,
hearts may be turned to honour what is just and true,
compassionate and constructive.
We pray that in all areas
where there is corruption, deceit or distrust,
consciences may be sensitised afresh
to know what is right and strive towards it.

Silence

You are the one true God:
and we worship you.

Lord of life, we pray for the streets
and places of work we represent.
May they be places where the truth of your being
is proclaimed daily by the way we live
and handle the everyday situations, through your leading.

May our words and actions speak of your faithful love,
your graciousness and your purity.

Silence

You are the one true God:
and we worship you.

Lord of life,
we pray for all who feel out of their depth,
all who are drowning in their pain, sorrow or guilt.
Set them free, O God, and save them,
support them to a place of safety
and fix their feet on the solid rock of your love.

Silence

You are the one true God:
and we worship you.

Lord of life, we pray for those who have died
and now see you as you really are.
We ask for mercy and forgiveness,
and commend them to your keeping for ever.

Silence

You are the one true God:
and we worship you.

Lord of life, your love for us is so great
and our love for you so small.
Thank you for accepting what we are able to offer;
and ignite us to a blaze of love.

Merciful Father,
accept these prayers
for the sake of your Son,
our Saviour Jesus Christ. Amen.

ASCENSION DAY

*Having bought back our freedom with the giving of his life,
Jesus enters into the full glory to which he is entitled.*

As we celebrate together, let us pray together.

God of love, as we celebrate this festival
of Jesus' entry into heaven as Saviour and Lord,
we pray for unity in the Church
and reconciliation and renewed vision.

Silence

Both heaven and earth:
are full of God's glory.

As we recall the shout of praise in heaven
as the Lamb of God appears,
we pray for all who are hailed as heroes
and given great honour on earth;
for all who worship anyone or anything
other than the true God.

Silence

Both heaven and earth:
are full of God's glory.

We pray for all farewells and homecomings
among our families and in our community,
and for all who have lost touch with loved ones
and long for reunion.

Silence

Both heaven and earth:
are full of God's glory.

We pray for those who are full of tears,
and cannot imagine being happy again;

we pray for the hardened and callous,
whose inner hurts have never yet been healed.
We pray for wholeness and comfort and new life.

Silence

Both heaven and earth:
are full of God's glory.

We commend to your eternal love
those we remember who have died,
and we pray too for those
who miss their physical presence.

Silence

Both heaven and earth:
are full of God's glory.

We praise and bless you, God of our making,
for the way you draw us deeper
into the meaning of life.

Merciful Father,
accept these prayers
for the sake of your Son,
our Saviour Jesus Christ. Amen.

SEVENTH SUNDAY OF EASTER

*God's glory is often revealed in the context of
suffering and failure in the world's eyes.*

As the Church of God,
let us be still, and pray together.

God of glory,
may your light shine in our church community
as you work among us and bless us with your presence;
we offer you the gifts you have given us
and our various ministries;
we offer you ourselves, in the area you have placed us.

Silence

Holy God:
may we live with your life in us.

God of glory,
may the whole world come to know you
and give you honour and praise.
Encourage us all to stand up to the devil, when he prowls,
firm in our faith, and strengthened with your power.
May your kingdom come and your will be done.

Silence

Holy God:
may we live with your life in us.

God of glory,
may our homes, schools, shops, offices and factories
become places where your glory is seen and experienced
in the ordinary things, the everyday routines,
the pots and pans of life.
Fill us to overflowing with ongoing thankfulness
both in the sunlight and in the storm.

Silence

Holy God:
may we live with your life in us.

God of glory,
with your special affection
for the discarded and marginalised,
the weak and the vulnerable,
we pray for all those who find life an exhausting struggle
or who long for some respite from pain or depression.
Support them in their troubles,
bring healing and reassurance,
and touch them with the gentleness of your peace.

Silence

Holy God:
may we live with your life in us.

God of glory,
teach us to understand death
in the context of your eternity,
so that our fears are calmed as we approach it.
Welcome with merciful love those who have recently died
and shelter their loved ones, too,
in the shadow of your wings.

Silence

Holy God:
may we live with your life in us.

God of glory, we thank you
that through your ascension into heaven
the way was open for us to receive the Holy Spirit.
Prepare our hearts each day to welcome you.

Merciful Father,
accept these prayers
for the sake of your Son,
our Saviour Jesus Christ. Amen.

PENTECOST

*With great power the Spirit of God is
poured out on the expectant disciples.*

As the body of Christ,
in the power of the Spirit,
let us pray.

For a fresh outpouring of the Holy Spirit
on the people of God all over the world,
and in all worship traditions.
For a readiness to be changed and made new;
for a softening of the ground of our hearts
to receive without fear.

Silence

With our whole selves we pray:
come, Holy Spirit of God.

For all the peoples of the earth
to know you and honour your name.
For the healing of the nations
and a new thirst for righteousness and purity
at every level and in every aspect of society.
For a dissatisfaction with the pursuit of pleasure
and all that distracts us from our true calling.

Silence

With our whole selves we pray:
come, Holy Spirit of God.

For the grace and power to live out our faith
in the real and challenging world,
among those we meet and eat with,
whose lives we share,
without compromising that calling
to be the body of Christ,
living God's integrity and purity,
forgiveness and love.

Silence

With our whole selves we pray:
come, Holy Spirit of God.

For those whose lives feel empty or cheated,
or filled with pain, or worry or guilt.
For all whose hopes and dreams are in tatters;
all who are in any way imprisoned.

Silence

With our whole selves we pray:
come, Holy Spirit of God.

For those who walk the dark journey of death
and all who have come through it
into your presence;
for mourners distressed by regrets
or angry with God at their loss.

Silence

With our whole selves we pray:
come, Holy Spirit of God.

For all you have in store for us, we thank you;
we look forward to walking into the future
of your promise, alive with your life.

Merciful Father,
**accept these prayers
for the sake of your Son,
our Saviour Jesus Christ. Amen.**

TRINITY SUNDAY

*The mystery of God – Creator, Redeemer and
Sanctifier all at once – is beyond our human
understanding, yet closer to us than breathing.*

Called by the great God we worship,
let us pray fervently for the Church and for the world.

We bring before you, O God,
the needs of the Church,
in its weakness and its potential;
revive and refresh us, teach and direct us,
inspire all who preach, teach and gossip the good news,
and uphold all who suffer for their faith in any way.

Silence

God of mystery and compassion:
you know us and you love us.

We bring before you, O God,
the particular problems of our age and our culture;
renew in us a commitment to community
and mutual trust,
give a sense of value to all
who despise others and themselves;
protect the vulnerable and sensitise the hearts
of all who have become anaesthetised
by images of violence.

Silence

God of mystery and compassion:
you know us and you love us.

We bring before you, O God,
the nurturing of our children and young people,
in homes and parenting, schools and teaching,
in the expectations, pressures and dangers,
in the hopes and possibilities for good.

Silence

God of mystery and compassion:
you know us and you love us.

We bring before you, O God,
the hungry and malnourished, the greedy and complacent;
those who are ill and those who care for them;
the unhappy and those who comfort them;
all who are undergoing surgery or painful treatment,
and all who have no one to turn to.

Silence

God of mystery and compassion:
you know us and you love us.

We bring before you, O God,
those who have died in faith
and will now see you face to face;
those for whom death speaks of fear or annihilation,
and those who are unprepared to meet you.

Silence

God of mystery and compassion:
you know us and you love us.

We bring before you, O God,
our lives and all that we are,
including our successes and our failures;
we thank you for the gift of life
and ask that we may get to know you more deeply
day after day.

Merciful Father,
accept these prayers
for the sake of your Son,
our Saviour Jesus Christ. Amen.

PROPER 4

Sunday between 29 May and 4 June inclusive (if after Trinity Sunday)

Wise listeners build their lives up
on the strong rock of the word of God.

As the community of God's people,
let us focus our attention and still our bodies to pray.

Father, we have heard your words and your challenge
to build our lives wisely on the bedrock of faith;
may all of us who profess to be Christians
act on what we have heard.
Bless and inspire all who preach and teach the faith
and make our worship pure and holy
and acceptable to you.

Silence

Lord God of wisdom:
you give us the word of life.

Father, we are conscious of the double standards
and inconsistencies in our world,
and ask for hearts to be opened to hear you
and recognise the wisdom of your law of love.
We ask you to strengthen and encourage each attempt
to govern with your principles,
and deal justly with your sense of mercy.

Silence

Lord God of wisdom:
you give us the word of life.

Father, we want to take more seriously
our community commitment to our children.
Show us what needs to be started,
developed or changed in our attitudes to one another,
and in the way we help one another's faith to grow.

Silence

Lord God of wisdom:
you give us the word of life.

Father, the needs and concerns of all who suffer
are our concern, through love.
May we strive to address
the imprisoning poverty and hunger
of much of our world,
and involve ourselves in the comfort, help and healing
we ask of you.

Silence

Lord God of wisdom:
you give us the word of life.

Father, we commend to your love and mercy
those who have died to this earthly life.
We thank you for lives well lived and love shared.
Bring them, and us in our turn, safely to heaven.

Silence

Lord God of wisdom:
you give us the word of life.

Father, we thank you that we can build strong lives
on the rock of Christ;
build us up in your love and wisdom.

Merciful Father,
**accept these prayers
for the sake of your Son,
our Saviour Jesus Christ. Amen.**

PROPER 5

Sunday between 5 and 11 June inclusive (if after Trinity Sunday)

*Jesus' life of healing and compassion acts out God's
desire for mercy rather than empty sacrifice.*

Come, let us return to the Lord who loves us,
and pray to him now.

God of truth, we pray that your Church
may be led into the way of truth
and an ever-deepening understanding
of your nature and your will.
We pray for our leaders and teachers and pastors;
we pray for right priorities
and a softening of the ground of our hearts.

Silence

Come:
let us return to the Lord.

God of power, we pray for those with authority,
influence and power in our world;
for all who are easily led,
often against their conscience;
we pray for a re-aligning of right values
and a reawakening of mutual respect and trust.

Silence

Come:
let us return to the Lord.

God of loving kindness,
watch over our homes and families,
our friends and neighbours;
we pray too for those who wish us harm
and those we find it difficult to love;
we pray for more of you in all our relationships.

Silence

Come:
let us return to the Lord.

God of mercy and compassion,
we bring to you all those who, through illness,
accident, age, abuse or human weakness,
are suffering as we gather here.
Gather them up in your love
and give your healing, your strength and courage,
your hope and wholeness.
We make ourselves available
as channels of your love.

Silence

Come:
let us return to the Lord.

God of eternity,
in whom there is no beginning or end,
welcome into your presence those who have died,
and give comfort to those
who miss their earthly company.
Give us all a greater understanding
of the new life you offer.

Silence

Come:
let us return to the Lord.

God of glory,
we worship you with all creation.
We worship you with the sun and stars,
all land, sea and sky, all that grows and moves,
all that is still and reflective, all that breathes.

Merciful Father,
accept these prayers
for the sake of your Son,
our Saviour Jesus Christ. Amen.

PROPER 6
Sunday between 12 and 18 June inclusive (if after Trinity Sunday)

*Jesus sends his ambassadors out to proclaim God's
kingdom and bring hope and peace of mind to
the harassed and lost in every age.*

Let us join in praying together with all God's people
to the Lord of the harvest.

Heavenly Father, we thank you for the gift of life,
and above all for your love in dying for us
who so often act as your enemies.
Break down any barriers
which prevent us from being at peace with you,
and fill your Church with love
for all who do not yet know your peace.

Silence

You, O Lord:
you are our hope and joy.

Father, we thank you for the diversity
and richness of our world,
for the natural goodness of many,
and the innocence of the very young.
We pray for all victims of our world's mistakes and evils,
and ask your guidance and courage
for our leaders and advisers.

Silence

You, O Lord:
you are our hope and joy.

Father, we thank you for the joy
of our families and friendships,
and the opportunities provided in our homes
for learning what real loving is all about.
We pray for those we love and worry about,

and those who love and worry about us,
commending one another to your keeping.

Silence

You, O Lord:
you are our hope and joy.

Father, we thank you for all the medical research
that has brought healing and quality of life to so many.
We pray for all who work in our hospitals,
hospices and clinics, and for all the patients in their care.
We pray for all who are harassed and worried,
and long for the peace of mind that eludes them.

Silence

You, O Lord:
you are our hope and joy.

Father, we thank you
for all who have lived your praise
and worked for the coming of your kingdom.
Receive into the joy of heaven
all who have died in faith,
whose strong hope in the eternal God
is not disappointed, but fulfilled.

Silence

You, O Lord:
you are our hope and joy.

Father, we thank you for all
who sense your calling and respond to it with joy.
We pray for still more workers in your harvest,
to gather in many to share the joy of your peace.

Merciful Father,
accept these prayers
for the sake of your Son,
our Saviour Jesus Christ. Amen.

PROPER 7

Sunday between 19 and 25 June inclusive (if after Trinity Sunday)

*When we are willing to take up our cross
with Jesus we will also know his risen life.*

Let us pray to our heavenly Father,
who is familiar with our world
and understands our humanity.
Lord of all, wherever Christians are ridiculed
or persecuted for their faith,
we ask your courage and inner strength;
wherever we are called to be your witnesses,
we ask for the grace to communicate your love.
Wherever love for you has grown cold
we ask to fan the flames again.

Silence

In Christ we can be dead to sin:
and alive to God.

Lord, wherever the human spirit
is ground down by oppression,
and wherever our silence allows injustice
and corruption to flourish,
we ask for deeper compassion and commitment;
we ask for our kingdoms to become your kingdoms,
and the desires of your heart to be ours.

Silence

In Christ we can be dead to sin:
and alive to God.

Lord of all, wherever families are struggling
to stay together,
and wherever there are ongoing arguments
and family feuds,
we ask your anointing for tranquillity and harmony.
Wherever children are unwanted and unloved,
neglected or in danger, we ask your protection and help.

Silence

In Christ we can be dead to sin:
and alive to God.

Lord, wherever bodies, minds or spirits
are wracked with pain,
or too weak or exhausted to pray,
we ask the bathing love of your presence,
and the practical caring of hands working in your name.
Wherever there are doubts and the battle is strong,
we ask your empowering and clear guidance.

Silence

In Christ we can be dead to sin:
and alive to God.

Lord of all,
wherever the dying are anxious and afraid,
we ask your peace;
wherever the faithful have passed
from this life into eternity,
we commend them to your unchanging
and everlasting love.

Silence

In Christ we can be dead to sin:
and alive to God.

Wherever nature's beauty or the daily miracles around us
alert us to see your face, we thank you for the grace
to live this resurrection life.

Merciful Father,
accept these prayers
for the sake of your Son,
our Saviour Jesus Christ. Amen.

PROPER 8

Sunday between 26 June and 2 July inclusive

As Christ's people we are no longer slaves to sin,
but available for righteousness.

Let us focus our bodies, minds, hearts and wills
as we pray to the God of all creation.

Holy God, you are the focus of our love and worship,
because you alone are the Lord
who has made us and rescued us.
May we not return to the slavery of sin
but live in your freedom, serving you with joy,
in thankfulness for all you have done for us.

Silence

Heal us, Lord:
and use us to your glory.

Holy God, though the world may often reject you,
you never fail to believe in us all
and love us with tenderness.
We pray for all areas of conflict, deceit,
mismanagement and greed,
and for all who are drawn into the chaos of evil.

Silence

Heal us, Lord:
and use us to your glory.

Holy God, our daily lives provide such rich ground
for acts of loving kindness,
self-discipline and courage.
Remind us of the opportunities,
and strengthen us to use them.

Silence

Heal us, Lord:
and use us to your glory.

Holy God, we thank you for all
who lovingly look after those in nursing homes,
hospitals, nurseries and prisons,
and we pray for all who need such care
and rely on others' help.

Silence

Heal us, Lord:
and use us to your glory.

Holy God, we call to mind
those who have recently died
and thank you for each act of goodness in their lives.
Have mercy on them and forgive their failings,
so that they may share the joy of heaven for ever.

Silence

Heal us, Lord:
and use us to your glory.

Holy God, we thank you
for our human potential for good,
and for your gift of grace
that makes such goodness a real possibility.

Merciful Father,
accept these prayers
for the sake of your Son,
our Saviour Jesus Christ. Amen.

PROPER 9

Sunday between 3 and 9 July inclusive

To all who are weary with carrying heavy burdens in life,
Jesus offers rest for our souls and unthreatening relief.

Our loving God is here, attentive to his children.
Let us pray to him now.

Father, we pray that your Church
may always be open to receive your love;
keep us swept clear of pomposity,
complacency or self-righteousness;
let us come humbly and simply into your presence
and wait on you, knowing our dependence on you,
and rejoicing in it.

Silence

As you have called us:
Lord, we come to you.

Father, we pray for all world leaders
and their governments;
for the strength of authority
comes not through force and domination
but through co-operation and mutual respect;
we pray for greater consideration
of the needs of one another and of our planet,
and a desire to right past wrongs and injustices.

Silence

As you have called us:
Lord, we come to you.

Father, we pray for a growing maturity
in our thinking and our loving
that enables us to be childlike;
we pray for healing from all the damage
that prevents us from growing up;

we pray that our children in this church
may be helped to grow strong,
and we thank you for all we learn from them.

Silence

As you have called us:
Lord, we come to you.

Father, we pray for all who cry out for rest and relief,
all who are carrying terrible burdens
that weigh them down,
all whose poverty denies them the chance of healing,
all whose wealth denies them
the chance of knowing their need of you.

Silence

As you have called us:
Lord, we come to you.

Father, we pray for those who die unprepared to meet you,
and for all who have died recently,
both those well-known to us
and those dying unknown and unnoticed
all over the world.

Silence

As you have called us:
Lord, we come to you.

Father, we thank you for your gentleness and humility,
which puts our pride and vanity to shame.
Teach us to trust more and more in your truth,
discarding what the world considers essential
and rejoicing in your freedom.

Merciful Father,
**accept these prayers
for the sake of your Son,
our Saviour Jesus Christ. Amen.**

PROPER 10

Sunday between 10 and 16 July inclusive

Seed of God's word, sown in good soil,
watered by his rain and warmed by his sunlight,
produces a good crop of spiritual fruit.

Gathered together as the people of God,
and attentive to his will, let us pray.

Heavenly Father, may your words of truth
take root in our hearts and grow to rich maturity.
May we hear your will for us and act upon it;
may we take seriously our responsibility
to encourage and nurture one another in faith
at every age and every stage.

Silence

Eternal truth, living God:
your word is life and strength.

Heavenly Father, may every act of selfless giving
and every search for truth be richly blessed and rewarded;
Disturb assumptions and lead
many to ponder more deeply
the spiritual dimension of their lives.
May the word of God reach all who are ready to receive it,
and let us set no boundaries here as to who they might be.

Silence

Eternal truth, living God:
your word is life and strength.

Heavenly Father, make our homes
places of love and growth,
welcoming to all who visit them,
and accepting and forgiving to all who are nurtured there.
Help us through the quarrels and heartaches
and remind us to honour one another
as your cherished ones.

Silence

Eternal truth, living God:
your word is life and strength.

Heavenly Father, may all whose bodies,
souls or minds are aching
know the comforting and strengthening power
of your companionship, and the healing work of your love.
May we be more ready
to support and befriend one another
through the difficult times,
in the name and love of the God we worship.

Silence

Eternal truth, living God:
your word is life and strength.

Heavenly Father, we pray for all
who are making the journey through physical death,
as they put down earthly things
and wake to your presence.
Bring us all to share with them
your life in all its fullness.

Silence

Eternal truth, living God:
your word is life and strength.

Heavenly Father, the rain and sunshine,
the growing and harvesting,
sing to us of your faithful love,
and we offer you our thankful praise
for all your gifts to us.

Merciful Father,
accept these prayers
for the sake of your Son,
our Saviour Jesus Christ. Amen.

PROPER 11

Sunday between 14 and 23 July inclusive

*God's justice is always blended with mercy and
loving kindness, so that we have real hope.*

Let us draw near to the just and merciful God,
and pour out our concerns
for the Church and for the world.

Lord our God,
as we join the unending cycle of prayer on our planet,
turning through time and space,
we rejoice in your upholding, your mercy and forgiveness.
In all our small-mindedness we ask your inbreathing,
so that we learn to look with your vision
and act with your wideness of compassion.

Silence

God of mercy:
hear us as we pray.

Lord our God,
be present at all meetings and negotiations,
where feelings run high,
and many lives are profoundly affected
by the decisions made.
We pray for real communication
which listens to needs and appreciates difficulties,
so that we may live on this earth together
in harmony and peace.

Silence

God of mercy:
hear us as we pray.

Lord our God,
we pray for this neighbourhood
and the particular problems it has;

for communities split apart by conflict
or crushed by tragedy;
we pray for those involved with court proceedings;
may our judicial system uphold your principle
of justice with mercy.

Silence

God of mercy:
hear us as we pray.

Lord our God,
we pray for those who have a raw deal in this life;
for those with ongoing health problems,
and all who are caught up in war and deprivation.
We pray for a just and realistic sharing of our resources,
and courage, support and healing for all who suffer.

Silence

God of mercy:
hear us as we pray.

Lord our God, we pray for those who have died
and now see their lives as they really are;
we pray for your mercy on them,
and thank you for all their acts of goodness and love.

Silence

God of mercy:
hear us as we pray.

Lord our God,
in all the events and phases of our life
we give you thanks
for your steadfast and unchanging love
which sustains and directs us.

Merciful Father,
accept these prayers
for the sake of your Son,
our Saviour Jesus Christ. Amen.

PROPER 12

Sunday between 24 and 30 July inclusive

*Jesus, the teacher, enables the ordinary,
unlearned people to understand God's wisdom –
the eternal laws of his Father's kingdom.*

May the Spirit pray through us
as we try to put into words the longings of our hearts
for the Church and for the world.

Father, we thank you
for all who have helped us to pray
and to grasp something of your great love and power.
We ask your blessing and empowering
for all who teach and minister in your name;
we ask for our Sunday worship to be an overflowing
of our daily walk with you,
an expression of our deepening love.

Silence

Lord of all creation:
teach us your ways.

Father, we thank you for the beauty and diversity
of the created world we inhabit.
We ask for the wisdom to tend it carefully,
respecting the natural laws and sharing the resources,
listening to the weak as well as the strident,
the poor as well as the affluent and powerful.

Silence

Lord of all creation:
teach us your ways.

Father, we thank you
for the candour and innocence of the very young,
and for the joy of friendship;
for all with whom we share our daily life,
and those we love but seldom meet.
We ask for hearts that are skilled in listening,

so that we discern and respond to the real agendas,
and remember that a conversation is a two-way event.

Silence

Lord of all creation:
teach us your ways.

Father, we thank you
for the advances in medical knowledge
and the hope of new treatments for many diseases.
We pray for all in medical research
and all whose lives are crippled or disadvantaged
by illness, frailty or damage.
Give comfort and reassurance,
healing, wholeness and peace.

Silence

Lord of all creation:
teach us your ways.

Father, we call to mind
all those we have known and loved
who lived among us and now have died.
We pray for all who made that journey
unnoticed and alone.
We ask that they may all know your mercy
and the everlasting peace and joy of heaven.

Silence

Lord of all creation:
teach us your ways.

Father, we thank you for your wisdom and truth,
your understanding and generosity.
We acknowledge our total dependence on you,
and praise you for providing us with all we need.

Merciful Father,
**accept these prayers
for the sake of your Son,
our Saviour Jesus Christ. Amen.**

PROPER 13

Sunday between 31 July and 6 August inclusive

*God feeds all who come to him hungry, and we,
as the Church, are expected to share in that work.*

We have gathered here
to meet with our God in worship.
Let us pray to him now.

Lord, awaken in us our need of you
and make us hungry and thirsty for you,
both as individuals and as the Church of God.
Let no other issues side-track us from seeking you,
and increase our love and compassion
so that we long to serve out your love
to the world around us.

Silence

Bread of heaven:
on you we feed.

Lord, allow our world to see the true value of things,
so that the worthless and dangerous is unmasked
and real needs acknowledged.
Guide our leaders in wisdom and integrity,
and enable us all to co-operate in proper care
and stewardship of the world's resources.

Silence

Bread of heaven:
on you we feed.

Lord, as we eat our food this week,
remind us of your spiritual feeding.
May the meals we prepare and eat together
be opportunities for drawing closer
to one another and to you.

Silence

Bread of heaven:
on you we feed.

Lord, we pray for all who need medical treatment
or are waiting in pain for surgery.
We pray for those who have become addicted
and long to be set free.
We pray for all whose wrong choices
have ended in heartache, disillusion and despair.

Silence

Bread of heaven:
on you we feed.

Lord, welcome into your eternity
all who have spent their lives coming to you
and now come to be with you for ever.
Have mercy on all those approaching death
who do not know you
but reject what they imagine you to be.
May they respond to the true and living God
and know your love for ever.

Silence

Bread of heaven:
on you we feed.

Lord, thank you for feeding us
with spiritual food that satisfies our souls.

Merciful Father,
**accept these prayers
for the sake of your Son,
our Saviour Jesus Christ. Amen.**

PROPER 14

Sunday between 7 and 13 August inclusive

God is faithful to us through all the storms of life,
yet our faith in God is so very small.

Trusting in our faithful God, let us pray.

Faithful God, we pray for the gift
of deeper faith in you,
so that we trust you in a way
that alters our dependence on everything else,
and allows us clearer vision
as to the direction and role of the Church.
Remind us that it is your Church, and not ours;
your work, your power and your kingdom.

Silence

Lord our God:
let only your will be done.

Faithful God, as we call to mind
the stormy areas of our world,
the raging and the insecurity,
the confusion and bewilderment,
the restlessness and fear,
let your calming and reassuring presence
be sensed and recognised,
bringing peace and goodness,
righteousness and hope.

Silence

Lord our God:
let only your will be done.

Faithful God, come to us in the storms of life,
when we let one another down,
mishandle opportunities
and come to the end of our strength or patience;
and bless us with the love that never lets us down.

Silence

Lord our God:
let only your will be done.

Faithful God, we place into your loving keeping
all those who have died,
knowing their dependence on you
and your limitless mercy.
We thank you for them and their gifts to the world,
and ask that we may, in our turn,
come to you across the waters of death
and live in your company for ever.

Silence

Lord our God:
let only your will be done.

Faithful God, whose promises stand sure for ever,
we thank you for your patience with us
and your refusal to give up on us.

Merciful Father,
**accept these prayers
for the sake of your Son,
our Saviour Jesus Christ. Amen.**

PROPER 15

Sunday between 14 and 20 August inclusive

The good news of salvation is not limited to a particular group or nation but available for the whole world.

In faith let us pray to the God
who is Lord of all the earth.

Holy God, may the worship of your Church
throughout the world be attentive and expectant,
ready to be set on fire again and again
with the outrageous foolishness of loving,
without exceptions and without limits and without praise.

Silence

Servant God:
let us honour you with our lives.

Holy God, may all that encourages people
in goodness, honesty and compassion
be blessed and grow;
may all that encourages self-seeking and cruelty,
prejudice and deceit wither and be exposed
as the unsatisfying rubbish it is.
May we learn from one another's cultures
and respect one another's differences.

Silence

Servant God:
let us honour you with our lives.

Holy God, we thank you for the joy of human love,
and for all those among whom we live and work.
We pray particularly for loved ones
who worry us with their health,
or circumstances, or life direction.
We pray for those among our friends and families
who do not know you,
or whose faith has been shaken.

Silence

Servant God:
let us honour you with our lives.

Holy God, we pray for all whose backgrounds
make belief in a loving God laughable or terrifying.
We pray for all who suffer
mental or emotional anguish
and those who despair.
We pray for those facing another day of pain,
another day of hunger, another day of fear.

Silence

Servant God:
let us honour you with our lives.

Holy God, gather into your eternal kingdom
all who have come to the end of this earthly life
and rejoice to see you as you really are.
We remember all whom we love but can no longer see,
and thank you for your overarching love
and undergirding faithfulness to us.

Silence

Servant God:
let us honour you with our lives.

Holy God, we remember with gratitude
all who gave up so much
to bring the good news to our country,
and pray that with us it may continue to be spread
until the whole earth knows of your truth and love.

Merciful Father,
accept these prayers
for the sake of your Son,
our Saviour Jesus Christ. Amen.

PROPER 16

Sunday between 21 and 27 August inclusive

*The Church is the Body of Christ, built on strong rock
of faith and energised by the living Breath of God.*

Gathered as the Church of God,
members of the Body of Christ,
let us pray together.

Fill your Church, O Lord,
with life and energy, spiritual health and vitality.
As we feed on you, may we grow more like you;
may we exercise your loving,
minister with your tenderness,
serve with your humility and co-operate with your vision.

Silence

In you, O Lord:
is all meaning and truth.

Fill your world, O Lord, with wonder at creation,
recognition of our mutual human responsibility,
desire for reforming what is at fault,
and hope in the possibilities of living at peace
with God and with one another.

Silence

In you, O Lord:
is all meaning and truth.

Fill our homes and neighbourhoods, O Lord,
with the generosity and trust that allows space
but is always ready to encourage and support.
May we cherish our bodies, minds and spirits
as temples containing your Spirit,
and honour one another as people of your making.

Silence

In you, O Lord:
is all meaning and truth.

We pray for all who are ill at home or in hospital,
for all in emergency surgery or in casualty;
for those who have just discovered
that they have injuries or illnesses
that will change their lives.
We pray for the work of all who heal and comfort,
all who visit the sick and counsel the distressed.

Silence

In you, O Lord:
is all meaning and truth.

We pray for the dying and those who love them;
we pray for those who have completed this life
and have made the journey through death.
We pray for the work of those who comfort the bereaved.

Silence

In you, O Lord:
is all meaning and truth.

Fill our hearts, O Lord, with thankfulness and praise
as we recall your faithfulness and live in your love.

Merciful Father,
accept these prayers
for the sake of your Son,
our Saviour Jesus Christ. Amen.

PROPER 17

Sunday between 28 August and 3 September inclusive

As Jesus prepares for the necessary suffering of the cross,
he is tempted, through well-meaning friendship, to avoid it.

As followers of Jesus Christ,
let us pray to our loving Father in heaven.

Father, help us all in your Church
to understand what it really means to love and serve you.
At the times of testing, strengthen us,
at unexpected or undeserved suffering, support us,
at the end of our energy, revive us
and teach us through it all the inexplicable peace and joy
that comes from doing your will.

Silence

We look to the cross:
and see your love for us.

Father, have mercy on us for the misdirected use
of time, money and resources in this world.
In the struggle against evil and sin, empower us,
so that justice and righteousness are established,
upheld and celebrated,
as hearts rejoice in the freedom of all that is good.

Silence

We look to the cross:
and see your love for us.

Father, renew our commitment to your loving
in all our relationships, our work and our prayer.
In the hard choices, give us wisdom,
in the painful decisions, affirm us,
and may our words speak your truth,
whether that is to encourage,
to comfort or to challenge.

Silence

We look to the cross:
and see your love for us.

Father, bring healing and wholeness
to those who suffer, in body, mind or spirit.
In the sleepless nights and endless days of pain,
give the grace to persevere with patience,
and turn these dark times
into places of spiritual growth.

Silence

We look to the cross:
and see your love for us.

Father, may those who have died
rest in the eternal peace of your presence,
their burdens laid down and their suffering ended.

Silence

We look to the cross:
and see your love for us.

Father, the full extent of your love for us
is so much greater than we can ever imagine,
and in our love and thankfulness
we offer the praise of our lives.

Merciful Father,
accept these prayers
for the sake of your Son,
our Saviour Jesus Christ. Amen.

PROPER 18

Sunday between 4 and 10 September inclusive

*It is our responsibility to encourage and uphold one
another in living by the standard of real love.*

In our need and human weakness,
let us come to Almighty God with our prayers.

Unchanging God, change us from the heart
until the whole Church awakens to your love
that reaches out, nurtures and celebrates,
neither holding back from what is difficult,
nor rushing where angels fear to tread.
We pray for sensitivity and courage.

Silence

Lord, take us by the hand:
and lead us.

Almighty God, give us such love for the world
that we may pray with longing and desire,
'Your kingdom come.'
Give our leaders the grace to see
their work as service and their role as stewards;
and sharpen both the recognition of needs
and the commitment to just provision.

Silence

Lord, take us by the hand:
and lead us.

Merciful God, break all habits
of destructive behaviour
in our homes and families, our friendships
and in all the homes of this parish.
Develop our ability to celebrate what is good
and face what is not with honesty.

Silence

Lord, take us by the hand:
and lead us.

Healing God, lay your hands on those who suffer,
so that they may know the support of your presence
and find wholeness and peace in your love.
We pray especially for those who are locked
into the conviction
that they are beyond your forgiveness.
May they quickly discover
the freedom of your acceptance.

Silence

Lord, take us by the hand:
and lead us.

Eternal God, in your unchanging love
receive all those who have died in faith,
that they may rejoice in you for ever.

Silence

Lord, take us by the hand:
and lead us.

Gracious God, we thank you for providing us
with a sure hope in which we can face the worst
and not be overwhelmed.

Merciful Father,
accept these prayers
for the sake of your Son,
our Saviour Jesus Christ. Amen.

PROPER 19

Sunday between 11 and 17 September inclusive

Forgiving is a natural result of loving,
so it is not an option for us but a command.

In the knowledge of all God has done for us,
let us bring to him our concerns
for the Church and for the world.

Thank you, Father, for the love
which forgives again and again,
and is prepared to trust us
with the care of your people
even after we have let you down many times.
Teach us to minister to one another's needs
with compassion, sensitivity and discipline,
so that all are affirmed and encouraged.

Silence

The Lord is full of compassion:
his love lasts for ever.

Thank you, Father, for the order and variety,
simplicity and complexity of this universe.
Thank you for all that humankind is able to do;
may all these gifts be used wisely and well,
for the good of all, including those as yet unborn.

Silence

The Lord is full of compassion:
his love lasts for ever.

Thank you, Father, for what we have been forgiven
and for the opportunities we have each day
to learn the joy of forgiving others.
Smash through our self-righteousness
and keep us learning in humility at your feet.

Silence

The Lord is full of compassion:
his love lasts for ever.

Thank you, Father, for all those who care for the sick,
the unstable, the ungrateful and the difficult.
We pray for all who are on the receiving end
of hate, deceit, suspicion or abuse,
and for those who cause others pain
and distress of any kind.
We pray for your healing and transforming.

Silence

The Lord is full of compassion:
his love lasts for ever.

Thank you, Father, for those whose living and dying
has taught us much about love.
Freed from their pain and restrictions of age or injury,
may they enjoy for ever the life of heaven.

Silence

The Lord is full of compassion:
his love lasts for ever.

Thank you, Father, for disturbing our complacency
and challenging us to move forward with you,
assured of your company and your love.

Merciful Father,
accept these prayers
for the sake of your Son,
our Saviour Jesus Christ. Amen.

PROPER 20

Sunday between 18 and 24 September inclusive

*We have no right to be envious at the generosity
and mercy God shows to others.*

Let us come with openness to express our concerns
for the Church and the world,
to the God of compassion and gracious understanding.

Loving Father, whenever we start to get offended
by your generosity or open-mindedness,
give us the grace to repent and join your rejoicing.
Guard the Church against self-righteousness
and all rules and limits which you would not own,
but keep always before us the rule of love.

Silence

Not our will:
but your will, Lord, be done.

Loving Father, increase in us love
not only for the victims but for the perpetrators
of evil and violence in our world;
for all governments
which run on corruption and fear.
We pray for a change of heart and attitude,
an awakening to a better way of living,
and the courage to reject wrong principles.

Silence

Not our will:
but your will, Lord, be done.

Loving Father,
may our closeness to family and friends
make us never exclusive, shutting others out,
but always inclusive, welcoming others in.
Encourage us in outgoing hospitality

and keep us from becoming
possessive with those we love.

Silence

Not our will:
but your will, Lord, be done.

Loving Father, we pray for all offenders in prison,
that on release they will not re-offend
but find enough support
to start a new life in the community.
We pray for all who are vulnerable
and unable to cope with the demands of life,
for alcoholics, drug addicts
and all who are sick in mind.
We pray for proper, compassionate help for them.

Silence

Not our will:
but your will, Lord, be done.

Loving Father, we pray for those
who have died alone, unmourned and unnoticed.
We pray for those who have committed suicide
or died in accidents of their own making.
We commend them to your merciful love.

Silence

Not our will:
but your will, Lord, be done.

Loving Father, thank you for helping us to pray;
deepen our loving
so that as we pray through this week
we may do it with your heart of compassion.

Merciful Father,
**accept these prayers
for the sake of your Son,
our Saviour Jesus Christ. Amen.**

PROPER 21

Sunday between 25 September and 1 October inclusive

God longs for us to die to sin and live,
but it has to be our choice, too.

God has called us;
as we gather in his name let us bring to him our prayers
which come from our love and concern.

Lord, we thank you for all the help and encouragement
we are given from the Church –
from its worship, teaching and fellowship;
from its faithfulness in prayer.
Bless and further all loving ministry
in word and sacrament throughout the world Church;
inspire us all to want your will and to do it.

Silence

O God, work in us:
inspiring both will and deed.

Lord, we pray for the world,
where the misery and tragedy of wrong choices
grieves your heart of love.
Let there be wisdom and compassion
in all negotiations and decisions;
let there be humility in leadership
and responsibility for right action shared by all.

Silence

O God, work in us:
inspiring both will and deed.

Lord, we bring to you the joys and worries,
the frustrations and accomplishments of this week
in the lives we have met and shared.
As we pray, let your light shine into all these lives
for fresh directing and lasting good.

Silence

O God, work in us:
inspiring both will and deed.

Lord, we bring to you those we know
who are ill or suffering in any way.
Give them healing, restore them
in body, mind and spirit,
and provide them with your indwelling.

Silence

O God, work in us:
inspiring both will and deed.

Lord, we remember in your presence
all those who have died,
and particularly those we have known and loved.
Thank you for them,
and thank you for your promise
of eternal life and peace.
May we comfort one another through your love.

Silence

O God, work in us:
inspiring both will and deed.

Lord, we thank you for your offer
of life in all its abundance;
may we accept it with joy every day of our life.

Merciful Father,
accept these prayers
for the sake of your Son,
our Saviour Jesus Christ. Amen.

PROPER 22

Sunday between 2 and 8 October inclusive

*God does everything possible for our spiritual
growth and well-being, but still we can
choose hostility and rejection.*

Let us pray trustfully to the God
who has loved us into being
and cherished us all our life.

Loving God, guide your Church
into ways of spiritual beauty and gracious wisdom.
May your word be spoken out with passion
and heard with humility and joy.
Sustain and feed us so that we bear fruit in abundance.

Silence

Root your people:
firmly in your love.

Loving God, may justice and righteousness
flourish in this neighbourhood, this country, this world.
Bless those who work to right what is wrong
and mediate where there is conflict.
Raise up leaders who are happy to serve
and protect them from power's corruption.

Silence

Root your people:
firmly in your love.

Loving God, we thank you
for the nurturing we have received,
and pray for our children and young people as they grow.
Protect them from evil and strengthen them in faith;
may they continue to be yours for ever.

Silence

Root your people:
firmly in your love.

Loving God, give comfort and healing to all
who are in any kind of need, sorrow or pain.
May they sense your reassuring presence
and know that you are there with them,
wherever their journey takes them.

Silence

Root your people:
firmly in your love.

Loving God, we pray for those
who have died to this earthly life,
and now see you face to face.
We remember your mercy
and commit our loved ones
to the safety of your keeping.

Silence

Root your people:
firmly in your love.

Loving God, we thank you for all the care
and attention that you lavish on us;
make us worthy of our calling
and continue your ongoing work in us.

Merciful Father,
accept these prayers
for the sake of your Son,
our Saviour Jesus Christ. Amen.

PROPER 23

Sunday between 9 and 15 October inclusive

We are all invited to God's wedding banquet; in accepting
we must allow the rags of our old life to be exchanged
for the freely given robes of holiness and right living.

Invited by our God, we have gathered here.
Let us now voice our prayers
for the Church and for the world.

Father, when either the traditional or the progressive
blinds us to the truth of your will,
clear our vision and speak through our prejudices
until we are once again open to your changing.
May we be, before anything else, your people,
sharing your concerns and desires.

Silence

As you have called us:
Lord, we come.

Father, we recognise how powerful
the influences are in our world
which distract many and lead away from your truth.
We pray for the quiet whisper of your wisdom
to be noticed and acknowledged in many lives;
we pray for widespread discipline of the heart,
a new openness to generosity of spirit.

Silence

As you have called us:
Lord, we come.

Father, may our homes and daily schedules
be part of the territory of your kingdom,
where it is your will which guides
and your love which rules.

Silence

As you have called us:
Lord, we come.

Father, our hearts rail against the cruelty
and unfairness of suffering and disease,
and we kneel now alongside all in pain
and weep with them, crying out to you
for comfort and the healing of your love.
For you are no bringer of evil to our lives,
but share our sorrow and give us the grace to bear it.

Silence

As you have called us:
Lord, we come.

Father, as death takes from us those we love
and we find it hard to live without them,
take from us all bitterness of heart and
let us share with them the peace you give
over which death has no power at all.

Silence

As you have called us:
Lord, we come.

Father, it is such an honour
to be invited to your banquet;
make us worthy of our calling.

Merciful Father,
accept these prayers
for the sake of your Son,
our Saviour Jesus Christ. Amen.

PROPER 24

Sunday between 16 and 22 October inclusive

*All leaders and rulers are subject to the ultimate
authority and power of God, the living truth.*

Let us focus our gaze on the great God of our making,
as we pour out to him our prayers.

Lord of all, give your Church such maturity and wisdom
that we may not be swayed from our purpose and calling
by trivialities or worldly pressures,
but know increasingly our dependence
on you in all things and proclaim your Gospel
with steadfastness and joy.

Silence

You, O Lord:
are the ground of our being.

Lord of all, give to all monarchs,
leaders and heads of state graciousness and integrity,
that all in power and authority
may undertake their duties in a spirit of humility;
that the oppressed may find a voice,
and the nations work together for the good of the world.

Silence

You, O Lord:
are the ground of our being.

Lord of all, give to our homes
and places of work and leisure your harmony and peace;
give us grace to respect one another and ourselves
in the way we talk and think, and in the way we behave.

Silence

You, O Lord:
are the ground of our being.

Lord of all, speak your peace into the hearts
of all who are agitated, anxious or confused.
Lay your hands of healing on all who are ill
and let them know your reassurance and love.

Silence

You, O Lord:
are the ground of our being.

Lord of all, welcome into your kingdom
all who have kept faith
and now can lay their burdens down.
May they rest in your peace for ever.

Silence

You, O Lord:
are the ground of our being.

Lord of all, the order and complexity of creation
sings your praise,
and we give voice to it now
as we offer you our song of lives rededicated
to the work of your kingdom.

Merciful Father,
**accept these prayers
for the sake of your Son,
our Saviour Jesus Christ. Amen.**

PROPER 25

Sunday between 23 and 29 October inclusive

We are to love God with our whole being,
and love others as much as we love ourselves.

In love and trust, let us pray to our God.

Holy God, give us the courage
to tell out your truth without fear,
and to work for your kingdom with joy.
Thank you for the support
and love of other Christians,
and the richness of our varied traditions.
May we focus our attention on you with such love
that all unnecessary divisions between us crumble.

Silence

You are the Lord:
there is no other.

Holy God, we pray for our law makers and keepers;
may our laws work to uphold what is just and true.
We pray that we may live
in Godly peace and goodwill through choice,
rather than through fear of punishment;
through the desire to live well,
rather than avoiding detection.

Silence

You are the Lord:
there is no other.

Holy God, in all our day-to-day living
may we reject deceit and flattery,
so that our motives and behaviour are honest,
and our love for one another clear as the day.

Silence

You are the Lord:
there is no other.

Holy God, we pray for all law breakers and their families;
for those in prison
and those returning to the community.
We pray for those imprisoned by guilt or shame,
or trapped by physical frailty, illness or paralysis.
We pray for those whose lives are tragically disrupted
by war and famine, poverty and disease.

Silence

You are the Lord:
there is no other.

Holy God, we remember those who,
dying in faith, rejoice to see you as you are.
We thank you for their example
and commend them to your peace for ever.

Silence

You are the Lord:
there is no other.

Holy God, we give you thanks for the love
poured out to us each moment of each day,
and ask of you the grace to live our gratitude
and give freely of what we have freely received.

Merciful Father,
**accept these prayers
for the sake of your Son,
our Saviour Jesus Christ. Amen.**

ALL SAINTS' DAY

Sunday between 30 October and 5 November inclusive

Lives that have shone with God's love on earth
are filled with joy as they see their Lord face to face.

Knowing our dependence on God in all things,
let us pray to him now.

Glorious God, as we celebrate the lives
of those Church members who have shone
with the brightness of your love,
we offer you ourselves and our lives
in fresh commitment
and conscious awareness of our need for you
in this parish and as individual Christians.

Silence

Just as I am:
I come.

Powerful God, may your kingdom of love and peace
be established in this world and grow.
We pray for both the influential and the ignored,
both the popular and the disliked,
both the ambitious and the vulnerable.
Teach us all your ways and your values.

Silence

Just as I am:
I come.

Loving God, we call to mind
our families and friends, neighbours and colleagues,
thanking you for all the loving care and forgiveness,
and asking your light to shine
in all areas of hurt and misunderstanding.

Silence

Just as I am:
I come.

Healing God, we bring to you
those whose lives are darkened by pain,
fear or weariness.
Come to our aid;
help us to bear what must be carried,
and take from us all resentment and bitterness,
replacing it with the abundance of peace.

Silence

Just as I am:
I come.

Eternal God, we thank you for all the saints –
those recognised by the Church
and those known only to a few, and to you.
We praise you for their example
and rejoice that they live in your heaven
with every tear wiped away.
In your mercy may all who have died in your friendship
know your lasting peace.

Silence

Just as I am:
I come.

Gracious God, you can take us as we are
and transform us by your life in us.
Clear our lives of all that is not of you,
so that we let your goodness
shine through the colours of our personalities
and gifts you have given us.

Merciful Father,
**accept these prayers
for the sake of your Son,
our Saviour Jesus Christ. Amen.**

FOURTH SUNDAY BEFORE ADVENT

Sunday between 30 October and 5 November inclusive*

* For use if the Feast of All Saints was celebrated on 1 November and alternative propers are needed.

*With God's light and truth to guide us, we shall be
brought safely through to the end of time.*

Let us focus our hearts and minds
on the living God as we pray.

Father, the seriousness of these prophecies
urges us to be attentive and work rigorously
at the direction the Church is facing.
Cleanse and purify your people from the heart, O God,
until we have the vulnerability and openness of children,
and the brokenness of a holy nation.

Silence

Cleanse us, O God:
and revive us.

Father, the wars and destructive conflicts of our own age
bring home to us the tragic consequences
of living by greed and ambition,
bitterness and revenge.
Heal whatever emotional damage
causes complex hostility
and teach us to live in peace together.

Silence

Cleanse us, O God:
and revive us.

Father, we are distressed by so many young lives
broken and distorted by abuse and neglect,
and the heartbreak of families split apart
by emotional conflicts and financial worries.

Strengthen our families and keep them safe,
protecting the children from long-term damage.

Silence

Cleanse us, O God:
and revive us.

Father, we long for the injustices
of global poverty and famine
to be righted, and the suffering spared;
for children the world over to have clean water to drink,
and for effective cures to be available, whatever the cost.

Silence

Cleanse us, O God:
and revive us.

Father, as many die young through hunger,
mismanagement of resources and unfair sharing,
we pray for the victims, and ask you to gather them
into the light and peace of heaven.

Silence

Cleanse us, O God:
and revive us.

Father, so much is entrusted to us;
may we act responsibly
and take notice of your warnings.

Merciful Father,
accept these prayers
for the sake of your Son,
our Saviour Jesus Christ. Amen.

THIRD SUNDAY BEFORE ADVENT

Sunday between 6 and 12 November inclusive

*We need to keep ourselves awake and prepared
so that the Day of the Lord does not come to us
as darkness rather than light.*

In the power of the Spirit,
let us pray to the Lord.

Heavenly Father, anoint your Church all over the world
with the oil of your Spirit, so that we burn brightly,
lighting the dark world with your love and truth.
Keep our church communities from error and sin,
and supply us all, through word and sacrament,
with all our souls require.

Silence

Waken us, Lord:
to understand your love.

Heavenly Father, take the false values of our world
and upend them;
take the oppressed and free them;
take the leaders and inspire them;
take the past and redeem it, the present and fill it,
the future and guide us in it.

Silence

Waken us, Lord:
to understand your love.

Heavenly Father, it is in our homes and daily tasks
that you train us in loving obedience.
We pray for those who have to live and work with us
and are familiar with our habits, gifts and faults.
May we make the most of the opportunities
to love, to forgive, to stand back and to reach out.

Silence

Waken us, Lord:
to understand your love.

Heavenly Father, as we pray for all who are ill
in body, mind or spirit,
surround them with your love and healing,
your reassurance and peace.
We pray for those
who are too weak or exhausted to pray,
but simply know they ache for your comfort.

Silence

Waken us, Lord:
to understand your love.

Heavenly Father, as real and living for the dead
as for those of us walking through time,
we commend to your mercy and love
those who have died in your faith and friendship;
may we all share in the joy
of Christ's coming in glory.

Silence

Waken us, Lord:
to understand your love.

Heavenly Father, all the resources for holiness
you lovingly provide,
and we thank you
for your ongoing and unlimited provision.

Merciful Father,
accept these prayers
for the sake of your Son,
our Saviour Jesus Christ. Amen.

SECOND SUNDAY BEFORE ADVENT

Sunday between 13 and 19 November inclusive

The Day of the Lord will hold terror for the wicked and unprepared, but rejoicing for those living in God's light.

Gathered as God's people, let us pray.

Holy God, if we are presuming on your mercy,
alert us and shatter our complacency;
if we are doubting your mercy,
affirm in us the reality of your forgiveness.
May we, as the Church, encourage and warn,
but never condemn;
acknowledge sin, but never judge.

Silence

Christ will come again:
make us ready to meet him.

Holy God, raise up prophets to speak out your truth,
and draw attention to whatever needs changing
in our world, our expectations and assumptions,
our management of resources and finances,
our systems of government and our attitudes.
May all peoples come to recognise your truth.

Silence

Christ will come again:
make us ready to meet him.

Holy God, fill our homes and places of work
with so much love that tensions
and barriers melt away,
conflicts are resolved
and troubles lightened by being lovingly shared.
Open our hearts to hope again
where we had given up.

Silence

Christ will come again:
make us ready to meet him.

Holy God, may all in misery and despair
turn to find you close beside them in their heartache,
not condemning but loving them in their pain.
May all who are locked in terror or guilt be set free,
and may those whom long-term illness wearies
be strengthened to persevere, freed from resentment.

Silence

Christ will come again:
make us ready to meet him.

Holy God, Lord of the living and the dead,
we commend to your mercy all who have died,
and thank you for that eternal healing
which frees us from all pain and suffering.

Silence

Christ will come again:
make us ready to meet him.

Holy God, we thank you for the gifts and talents
you have given us.
Give us the courage to use them
for the good of the world.

Merciful Father,
accept these prayers
for the sake of your Son,
our Saviour Jesus Christ. Amen.

CHRIST THE KING

Sunday between 20 and 26 November inclusive

In total humility, at one with the least of his people,
Jesus, the Messiah or Christ, reigns as King,
with full authority and honour for eternity.

Let us humble ourselves in the presence of God
and pray to him for the Church and for the world.

Loving God, in all our ministry as the Church,
both laity and clergy,
on Sundays and on weekdays,
may we give glory to you
and further your kingdom.
Direct us to those who are searching
and give us the wisdom to know
how best to draw them to your love.

Silence

We are your people:
the sheep of your pasture.

Loving God, may we actively seek to do good,
to stand up against injustice and work for peace;
Lord, rid the world of the terrible evils
that result from unvoiced objections,
and unspoken misgivings.
Give us the courage to act as true citizens of heaven.

Silence

We are your people:
the sheep of your pasture.

Loving God, may the ways we manage our homes,
decisions, time and money be in keeping with our calling
as inheritors of the kingdom.
May your love undergird all our loving.

Silence

We are your people:
the sheep of your pasture.

Loving God, search for the lost,
bring back those who have strayed,
bind up the injured, and strengthen the weak;
help us all to share in this work of loving care.

Silence

We are your people:
the sheep of your pasture.

Loving God, welcome into your kingdom
all whose lives show them to be your servants,
whether or not they have known you by name.
Prepare us all to meet you with the confidence
of sins confessed and forgiven.

Silence

We are your people:
the sheep of your pasture.

Loving God, you have shown us such love and humility;
we offer you our thanks and praise.

Merciful Father,
**accept these prayers
for the sake of your Son,
our Saviour Jesus Christ. Amen.**

Year B

FIRST SUNDAY
OF ADVENT

Be alert and watchful; keep yourselves ready.

As we begin a new year in the life of the Church,
let us pray together to the God of our making.

Holy God, just as we are we come to you,
and ask for your kingdom to come in us
and in this place;
increase our faith and our love for you,
so that we may become the lights in darkness
that we are called to be.

Silence

O God, keep us awake to you:
and alive to your call.

Holy God, the signs in our world
of hate, distrust and greed
are shown to us clearly every day.
May we see with your eyes
the signs of hope and victory;
the opportunities for loving service,
for encouragement, reassurance and thanksgiving.

Silence

O God, keep us awake to you:
and alive to your call.

Holy God, bless the parenting and befriending
in all our relationships,
and increase our love for one another.
Give us the humility
to accept guidance and warnings, lovingly given,
and the courage to uphold one another in the faith.

Silence

O God, keep us awake to you:
and alive to your call.

Holy God, we bring to you in love
those who are weary with ongoing pain and weakness,
those who are frail with age and all who are vulnerable;
Pour your living strength into their lives
and protect them from all that is harmful.

Silence

O God, keep us awake to you:
and alive to your call.

Holy God, we pray for all
who have come to the end of their earthly life,
and for those whose lives feel empty without them.
Give comfort to the bereaved,
and everlasting peace to all who rest in your love.

Silence

O God, keep us awake to you:
and alive to your call.

Holy God, your faithful care
has brought us safely to this moment;
we thank you for your constant love, forgiveness,
strength and protection.

Merciful Father,
accept these prayers
for the sake of your Son,
our Saviour Jesus Christ. Amen.

SECOND SUNDAY
OF ADVENT

*John the Baptist prepares the way for the coming of the
Messiah by helping the people to realign their lives.*

As we gather expectantly in God's presence,
let us pray.

God of cleansing and liberating power,
give us the courage and perception
to see ourselves as we really are,
and repent of our sin;
may the whole Church be cleansed and renewed.

Silence

Come, O come, Emmanuel:
come and live in us.

God of wisdom and truth,
we pray for the world's leaders and all in authority,
that they may lead and govern wisely and honestly,
without corruption and for the common good.

Silence

Come, O come, Emmanuel:
come and live in us.

God of love and faithfulness,
may every family be surrounded and upheld
by your presence,
the conflicts healed and needs provided for,
and every act of kindness blessed.

Silence

Come, O come, Emmanuel:
come and live in us.

God of wholeness,
bring your reassurance and healing,
your hope and patience
to all who are suffering in any way;
bring freedom to all imprisoned by hate or guilt,
and a change of heart to all who need to forgive.

Silence

Come, O come, Emmanuel:
come and live in us.

God of unending life,
bring life in its fullness to us here,
and to those who have completed their time on earth.
May they know the freedom and joy of your heaven.

Silence

Come, O come, Emmanuel:
come and live in us.

God of warmth and brightness,
we praise you for all our many blessings,
and above all for coming to save us and set us free.

Merciful Father,
**accept these prayers
for the sake of your Son,
our Saviour Jesus Christ. Amen.**

THIRD SUNDAY OF ADVENT

In Jesus, God will be fulfilling the Messianic
prophecies about the promised Saviour.

Let us pray now to the living God,
who always keeps his promises,
and who knows us so well.

Loving Father, keep the Church faithful
in telling the good news, comforting the desolate,
actively loving justice
and drawing many to freedom
through the joy of your forgiveness.

Silence

Keep us faithful:
to your calling.

As the Church, we pray for the world,
that there may be integrity in leadership;
mercy and justice for rich and poor,
strong and weak;
that there may be peace among nations
and respect for all.

Silence

Keep us faithful:
to your calling.

As the family of believers, we pray
for those around us now and their needs;
and for the families we represent, and their needs.
May the love of Christ be shown in what we do
and how we speak and how we spend.

Silence

Keep us faithful:
to your calling.

In compassion we call to mind
all who are locked in physical or emotional pain,
all who are weighed down with worry,
guilt or despair.
Restore and refresh them, comfort and free them.

Silence

Keep us faithful:
to your calling.

As resurrection people, we commend to your love
those who have died to this earthly life.
May they, and we in our turn, experience for ever
the joy of your eternity.

Silence

Keep us faithful:
to your calling.

As followers of the living Christ,
we praise you for the prophecies fulfilled,
the promises honoured and the victory over evil
gloriously accomplished in him
to fill our lives with hope.

Merciful Father,
accept these prayers
for the sake of your Son,
our Saviour Jesus Christ. Amen.

FOURTH SUNDAY
OF ADVENT

*God's promised kingdom, announced both to King
David in ancient times and to Mary by the angel
Gabriel, will go on for ever.*

Gathered as the Church of God in this place,
let us pray together for the coming of the kingdom.

Lord of heaven, may the Church
be quiet enough to hear your voice,
humble enough to move your way,
and excited enough to spread the good news.

Silence

Living God:
let your kingdom come.

Lord of heaven, bless all who lead
with integrity and respect for others;
bless all in positions of authority
with humility and a sense of right;
may unjust practices be changed for good
and conflicts of great tension
be peacefully resolved.

Silence

Living God:
let your kingdom come.

Lord of heaven, make our homes
places of loving acceptance and developing faith;
teach us in all our friendships
to grow in generosity of spirit.

Silence

Living God:
let your kingdom come.

Lord of heaven, give patience and courage
to all who have to wait,
when the waiting is long and painful;
bring healing to all who are wounded,
whether physically or emotionally,
and give them assurance of your presence.

Silence

Living God:
let your kingdom come.

Lord of heaven, welcome into your eternity
those who have died to this life
and whose hope is in you.
Comfort those who mourn them
and reach into their pain with your love.

Silence

Living God:
let your kingdom come.

Lord of heaven, we thank you
for your faithful promise to us,
fulfilled in the coming of Jesus.
We welcome his kingship in our lives.

Merciful Father,
**accept these prayers
for the sake of your Son,
our Saviour Jesus Christ. Amen.**

CHRISTMAS DAY

Jesus Christ, the world's Saviour,
is here with us, born as a human baby.

As we gather to celebrate Christmas,
let us pray to the living God.

Lord God, thank you for our Church
and its people,
for our deacons, priests and bishops,
and all who pray.
Bless us all and strengthen us for your service
so we can touch the world with your love.

Silence

Holy God:
be born in us today.

Lord God, we thank you for our world
and all its beauty and blessing.
Teach us your ways, your love and your truth,
and let your kingdom grow and flourish.

Silence

Holy God:
be born in us today.

Lord God, we thank you for our families,
our neighbours and our friends,
for the happiness of human loving and sharing.
We pray for your blessing on all those we love,
whether present with us today or far away.

Silence

Holy God:
be born in us today.

Lord God, we thank you for health and strength,
and pray now for your help and healing
wherever people ache with pain and sorrow,
loneliness or fear.
Bless them in their need
and surround them with love.

Silence

Holy God:
be born in us today.

Lord God, we thank you for lives well lived,
and all who have guided us to you.
We pray for those who have died
and all for whom Christmas
sharpens the loss of loved ones.

Silence

Holy God:
be born in us today.

Lord God, we thank you for Christmas joy
and all the opportunities
to show our love for one another.
May our love, rooted in yours,
continue throughout the year.

Merciful Father,
accept these prayers
for the sake of your Son,
our Saviour Jesus Christ. Amen.

FIRST SUNDAY OF CHRISTMAS

Just as the angels said, a Saviour has been born for us.

As we celebrate Jesus being born among us,
let us pray in the presence of God.

That the Church may truly be the Body of Christ,
in loving servanthood, humility and availability;
that as pastors and teachers,
prophets and evangelists,
givers, carers and listeners,
the whole people of God may make Christ known.

Silence

O come:
let us adore him.

That the world God loved into being
and placed in our care
may be valued and respected,
and its resources fairly shared.

Silence

O come:
let us adore him.

That every family may be blessed and guided
through all the troubles and chances of life,
supporting one another in love
and forgiving one another every day.

Silence

O come:
let us adore him.

That there may be food and shelter enough
for each person on this earth,
comfort and practical help for all in need
and peace of mind for the worriers.

Silence

O come:
let us adore him.

That the dying may be at peace with God,
and that those of our loved ones
who are separated from us through death
may know the joy of heaven.

Silence

O come:
let us adore him.

That our praises and thankfulness
may be bright as meadow flowers
springing up wherever we walk
through this daily gift of life you provide.

Merciful Father,
accept these prayers
for the sake of your Son,
our Saviour Jesus Christ. Amen.

SECOND SUNDAY OF CHRISTMAS

The Word made flesh at Christmas was always
with God, always expressing his creative love.

Let us pray to the God
who loves us enough to come and save us.

We pray for the areas of the Church
which are weak in faith,
despondent or complacent;
that we may be recharged
with the power of your love,
reawakened to the good news,
and revitalised with the breath of the Spirit.

Silence

Living Word of God:
be spoken in our lives.

We pray for all areas of misunderstanding
between peoples and nations,
between needs and offers of help;
make us more ready to listen than instruct,
more ready to encourage than crush.

Silence

Living Word of God:
be spoken in our lives.

We pray for family feuds and difficulties
to be resolved and learnt from;
for the words we speak
to express love and respect,
with true charity and forgiveness.

Silence

Living Word of God:
be spoken in our lives.

We pray for all who have difficulty
hearing and speaking,
reading and writing;
for the oppressed and persecuted
whose voices are silenced,
and for all who have yet to hear
the good news of God's love.

Silence

Living Word of God:
be spoken in our lives.

We pray for those who have died
and those who are dying now;
may your Word of life
encourage them on their journey
and bring them safely to your eternal kingdom.

Silence

Living Word of God:
be spoken in our lives.

We pray in thankfulness
for the joy of human communication
and the privilege of communing with the living God.

Merciful Father,
accept these prayers
for the sake of your Son,
our Saviour Jesus Christ. Amen.

THE EPIPHANY

Jesus, the promised Messiah,
is shown to the Gentile world.

Let us pray to the God who loves us
and knows the terrain we travel.

We thank God for all those who brought
the good news of Jesus to us,
and all who nourish our faith today.
We pray that the whole people of God
may work in unity and openness
for the coming of God's kingdom.

Silence

Lord God:
we offer you ourselves.

We thank God that salvation is for all people,
and pray for a just and accepting world
where none is rejected, despised
or treated with contempt.

Silence

Lord God:
we offer you ourselves.

We thank God for the privilege of parenting
and of living in communities;
we pray that our homes and churches
may be welcoming and generous-hearted.

Silence

Lord God:
we offer you ourselves.

We thank God for all who care
with such thoughtfulness and practical loving

for those who are vulnerable,
and especially for the very young.
We pray for healing and wholeness,
peace of mind, protection and hope.

Silence

Lord God:
we offer you ourselves.

We thank God for all who have reached
the end of their earthly journey in faith,
that they may be welcomed into his eternity.
May we use the time left to us here
as good stewards of God's gifts.

Silence

Lord God:
we offer you ourselves.

We thank God for including us
in the plan of salvation,
and pray that we may be made worthy
of our calling.

Merciful Father,
**accept these prayers
for the sake of your Son,
our Saviour Jesus Christ. Amen**

THE BAPTISM OF CHRIST
FIRST SUNDAY OF EPIPHANY

*Through the Holy Spirit, Jesus is affirmed at his
Baptism as God's beloved Son, and we too are given
the Spirit of God which affirms us as God's
adopted daughters and sons.*

Let the Spirit of God in our hearts plead
for the Church and for the world.

Great God of all time and space,
fill the Church with such joy in believing
that all Christians overflow with love,
compassion, generosity and humility.
Let us walk your way and live your life.

Silence

May the Spirit of God:
fill us to overflowing.

Great God of power and justice,
fill the arenas of leadership and conflict
with sharpened consciences and with courage,
so that wise decisions are made,
needs met and wrongs righted.

Silence

May the Spirit of God:
fill us to overflowing.

Great God of gentleness and truth,
fill every home with new insight
and greater understanding.
Break down the divisive barriers
and build up our capacity to love.

Silence

May the Spirit of God:
fill us to overflowing.

Great God of attentive caring,
fill us with your practical compassion;
may all who suffer be heard,
comforted and cared for.
Heal both their situation and our hardness of heart.

Silence

May the Spirit of God:
fill us to overflowing.

Great God of unending being,
fill death with your life
and the dying with hope in you.
Prepare us all for life which lasts for ever.

Silence

May the Spirit of God:
fill us to overflowing.

Great God of all creation,
fill our mouths with praises
and our hearts with gratitude,
for all the glory that surrounds us.

Merciful Father,
accept these prayers
for the sake of your Son,
our Saviour Jesus Christ. Amen.

SECOND SUNDAY OF EPIPHANY

Jesus, the Christ,
unlocks the mysteries of God.

Let us pray to God,
who knows us better than we know ourselves,
and understands our world.

Lord, we know we are called
to be the Body of Christ;
make us worthy of that calling,
fervent in all our prayer and worship,
loving, faithful and honest in our lives,
so that the whole Church displays
what God is like.

Silence

Draw us closer:
closer to the heart of God.

We pray for the grace and wisdom
to care for this world we have been given as our home;
for perception in the difficult decisions,
and commitment to justice and peace.

Silence

Draw us closer:
closer to the heart of God.

We pray for the homes of this parish,
whose hopes and struggles, sorrows and fears
are already known to you.
May each household be blessed as we pray,
and may your love fill each life.

Silence

Draw us closer:
closer to the heart of God.

We pray for all who do not yet know you,
and all whose hearts are poisoned with hate
or weighed down with despair.
May your light scatter their darkness
and bring them hope and healing.

Silence

Draw us closer:
closer to the heart of God.

We pray for those who have died to this life
and are born into your heaven;
comfort those who miss their physical presence,
and bring us all to share in the fullness of your life.

Silence

Draw us closer:
closer to the heart of God.

We give you thanks for all that points us
towards the beauty of your love,
and draws us closer to you.

Merciful Father,
accept these prayers
for the sake of your Son,
our Saviour Jesus Christ. Amen.

THIRD SUNDAY OF EPIPHANY

Signs of glory lead us to believe
in Jesus as Lord and Saviour.

Drawn here by God,
let us bring to him our concerns
for the Church and the world.

We pray that the Church may be
a vibrant sign of God's life
in every generation and locality,
serving, listening and loving,
with the human face of ordinary people
lit with the brightness of God.

Silence

Direct us, Lord:
and we will follow.

We pray that the world's attention
may be refocused on what is of lasting value;
that in humility, all in authority
may hear the real needs,
honour them and act on them.

Silence

Direct us, Lord:
and we will follow.

We pray that all the households
and neighbourhoods represented here
may be alerted to the signs of glory around them
in the ordinary, daily miracles,
and come to welcome Jesus as Lord.

Silence

Direct us, Lord:
and we will follow.

We pray that all who are searching for God
may realise his closeness to them;
that wrong lives may be courageously righted,
and damaged lives and attitudes mended.

Silence

Direct us, Lord:
and we will follow.

We pray that the dying may turn to you
and be safely led through that last journey
to the peace and joy of eternal life.
We pray that we may all one day experience God's heaven.

Silence

Direct us, Lord:
and we will follow.

We pray that we may become increasingly aware
of God's amazing love for each of us,
until our hearts are overflowing
with thankfulness and praise.

Merciful Father,
accept these prayers
for the sake of your Son,
our Saviour Jesus Christ. Amen.

FOURTH SUNDAY OF EPIPHANY

*Jesus displays all the signs that mark
him out to be God's chosen One.*

As we gather in the presence
of the almighty, all-knowing God,
let us pray.

Holy God, great Spirit of all,
may the whole Church
honour and glorify your name
in daily lives, private prayer and public worship.

Silence

Holy God:
may your will be done.

May the whole world resound with your truth,
activate your compassion,
and be soaked in your peace.

Silence

Holy God:
may your will be done.

May all homes and households
make plenty of room for kindness and forgiveness;
clear the clutter of discontent,
and make us more thankful.

Silence

Holy God:
may your will be done.

May all who ache with sadness or physical pain
be comforted and cherished,
knowing your love for them.

Silence

Holy God:
may your will be done.

May the dying be surrounded with our prayers,
and those who have passed beyond death
remain safe for ever in your keeping.

Silence

Holy God:
may your will be done.

As we step into each new day
may our thanks and praise
give joy to the living God.

Merciful Father,
**accept these prayers
for the sake of your Son,
our Saviour Jesus Christ. Amen.**

PROPER 1

Sunday between 3 and 9 February inclusive
(if earlier than the Second Sunday before Lent)

The good news about God is far too good
to keep to ourselves.

We have gathered in the presence
of the one, holy God,
from whom all things take their being.
Let us pray to him now.

Wherever the sparkle of our vision has dulled,
set us glowing once again
at the very thought of you,
and restore our longing to draw closer to you
until our lives reflect your shining.

Silence

Who is the King of glory?
It is the Lord our God.

Wherever important and far-reaching decisions
need to be made,
wherever wrongs need righting
and justice needs to be restored,
breathe your wisdom and integrity
and let your kingdom come.

Silence

Who is the King of glory?
It is the Lord our God.

Wherever ongoing family conflicts need resolving,
wherever communication has broken down,
develop our capacity for unconditional loving,
and appreciation of every 'other'
as another child of your creating.

Silence

Who is the King of glory?
It is the Lord our God.

Wherever there is pain and suffering,
whether physical, emotional, mental or spiritual,
we pray for your fulsome healing,
and commit ourselves to be available
and ready to help.

Silence

Who is the King of glory?
It is the Lord our God.

As we call to mind those who have recently died
and those who will die today,
we pray for each of them,
that in their dying
they may find the greatest healing of all,
as they come into your holy presence for ever.

Silence

Who is the King of glory?
It is the Lord our God.

As we marvel afresh today
at your majesty and humility,
we thank you for the privilege of knowing you.

Merciful Father,
**accept these prayers
for the sake of your Son,
our Saviour Jesus Christ. Amen.**

PROPER 2

Sunday between 10 and 16 February inclusive
(if earlier than the Second Sunday before Lent)

Jesus wants to heal us to wholeness,
and to him no one is untouchable.

Let us come to ask for the healing touch of our God
in the Church and in the world.

God of humility,
your desire to save us
made you willing to share our human brokenness;
as the Body of Christ, may the Church share
that willingness to be vulnerable
in order to serve in love.

Silence

Good physician:
heal us.

God of power,
your authority is gracious and merciful;
inspire all those with authority in our world
to be prompted by you,
so that they open the way
for your kingdom to be established.

Silence

Good physician:
heal us.

God of accepting love,
drive far from our homes and communities
all rejection and devaluing;
all justification for barriers;
and give us the courage to reach out in love.

Silence

Good physician:
heal us.

God of compassion,
shock us into seeing more clearly
the ache of those
whom society rejects and overlooks;
the wounds of the discarded
and socially embarrassing.
May we reach out where others turn away.

Silence

Good physician:
heal us.

God of eternity,
we remember those who, healed for ever,
live with you in the fullness of life.
We pray that we too may come, by your grace,
to share the life which has no ending.

Silence

Good physician:
heal us.

Lord, we thank you for the extent of your love
which has no limits
and no exceptions.

Merciful Father,
accept these prayers
for the sake of your Son,
our Saviour Jesus Christ. Amen.

PROPER 3

Sunday between 17 and 23 February inclusive
(if earlier than the Second Sunday before Lent)

The Son of Man has authority on earth to forgive sins.

In the sure knowledge that God cherishes us,
let us pray to him now.

Heavenly Father, so full of forgiveness and mercy,
fill your Church to the brim with such holiness
that our understanding of your ways
deepens daily,
and all our work and worship glorifies your name.

Silence

Holy God:
release in us your praise.

Heavenly Father, so wise and perceptive,
take us to the heart of all conflicts,
and give us the grace to share in the healing
between factions and nations,
guided by your Spirit.

Silence

Holy God:
release in us your praise.

Heavenly Father, so comforting and kind,
help us to notice the needs around us,
in our families, friends and colleagues,
and respond to them in love.

Silence

Holy God:
release in us your praise.

Heavenly Father, so mindful of our pain,
we bring to you our sisters and brothers
whose joints are stiff
and whose bodies cannot move freely;
thank you for their courage and example;
we pray that you will help their spirits to dance
and fill their hearts with joy.

Silence

Holy God:
release in us your praise.

Heavenly Father, so welcoming to all,
we commend to your everlasting keeping
those who have recently died,
and those who mourn their going.

Silence

Holy God:
release in us your praise.

Heavenly Father, so faithful in your promises,
we thank you for the eternal 'Yes' of Christ
which echoes on through lives and generations.

Merciful Father,
accept these prayers
for the sake of your Son,
our Saviour Jesus Christ. Amen.

SECOND SUNDAY BEFORE LENT

Christ is the image of the unseen God.

Our God made us and our universe,
and delights in us.
Prompted by the Spirit of God in us,
let us pray.

We pray for the godly wisdom
that is touched by the beauty of creation,
delights in the diversity of people,
and warms to the possibilities
of co-operative prayer and work
for the coming of the kingdom.

Silence

Wise and holy God:
we are your children.

We pray for the godly wisdom
that, in observing symptoms, discerns causes
and responds to the real needs;
that strives not to control but enable,
not to manipulate but empower.

Silence

Wise and holy God:
we are your children.

We pray for the godly wisdom
that gives others both space and support,
that encourages and guides,
that knows when to speak
and when to be silent.

Silence

Wise and holy God:
we are your children.

We pray for the godly wisdom
that recognises the poverty of the rich
and the wealth among the poor;
that questions assumptions of worth
and cherishes those whom the world discards.

Silence

Wise and holy God:
we are your children.

We pray for the godly wisdom
that sees time in the context of eternity,
and death as the gateway to heaven.

Silence

Wise and holy God:
we are your children.

We pray for the godly wisdom
that lives simply and thankfully,
rejoicing in all that God is and does.

Merciful Father,
accept these prayers
for the sake of your Son,
our Saviour Jesus Christ. Amen.

SUNDAY BEFORE LENT

God's glory shows.

Let us pray to the God of glory,
revealed to us in his Son, Jesus.

Father, lengthen and deepen our attention span
as we, your people, listen to your beloved Son,
so that we do not fail to hear his will for us
or share his longing for the world to be saved.

Silence

Let us worship the Lord:
in the beauty of holiness.

Father, with such humility you entered the world
to save it through love's giving;
increase our desire to enter into
one another's suffering and hardship,
to share the world's resources fairly
with one another,
and recognise all humanity as brothers and sisters.

Silence

Let us worship the Lord:
in the beauty of holiness.

Father, let us not take one another for granted,
but wake each morning ready to notice the Christ
in each person we see and speak to;
and reverence your hidden presence
in all creation.

Silence

Let us worship the Lord:
in the beauty of holiness.

Father, in our prayer we stand alongside
all who are too weak to pray, or too confused;
may all who are suffering
sense your love and comfort,
and be given strength to persevere,
and peace of mind and spirit.

Silence

Let us worship the Lord:
in the beauty of holiness.

Father, we commend to your eternal presence
those who have recently died,
that they may rest in peace and rise in glory.

Silence

Let us worship the Lord:
in the beauty of holiness.

Father, thank you for providing always
the encouragement and inspiration we need
for the work you would have us do;
give us the grace to trust your will for us
and walk forward boldly in your company.

Merciful Father,
accept these prayers
for the sake of your Son,
our Saviour Jesus Christ. Amen.

FIRST SUNDAY
OF LENT

*After his Baptism Jesus is led by the Spirit into the
wilderness before returning to proclaim God's kingdom.*

As we begin this season of Lent,
let us move off into the desert
to communicate with our God.

Lord God, we come with all our muddled priorities,
and conflicting agendas,
to be made whole as the Body of Christ;
to renounce evil so as to be equipped
to announce the kingdom of peace.

Silence

With our God:
all things are possible.

Lord God, we come with the world's clamour
ringing in our ears,
with comfort zones beckoning us,
but the pain of injustice refusing to be shut out.
We come for the world's healing,
and for an end to all lying and deceit.

Silence

With our God:
all things are possible.

Lord God, we come with the demands
of home, family, work and expectations
warring in us for space and attention.
We come on behalf of those
too busy or too exhausted to pray;
that our daily lives may be washed in your peace,
ordered in holiness and lit up with your joy.

Silence

With our God:
all things are possible.

Lord God, we come with the needs and sorrows,
pain and suffering of our brothers and sisters
all over the world, who are aching –
physically, emotionally or spiritually;
we come to ask your comfort and healing love.

Silence

With our God:
all things are possible.

Lord God, we come to realign our lives
in the context of your eternity,
and to commend to your love our own loved ones
who have passed through earthly death
to the life which has no ending.

Silence

With our God:
all things are possible.

Lord God, we come with thankfulness
for the gift of life, and for the call to holiness.
Give us the grace to respond to your calling.

Merciful Father,
accept these prayers
for the sake of your Son,
our Saviour Jesus Christ. Amen.

SECOND SUNDAY OF LENT

A commitment of faith has far-reaching implications.

Let us pray to our God in faith,
knowing that he understands what is best for us.

Heavenly Father, increase our faith,
that everyone in your Church
may be more ready to trust you
and move forward with you
wherever you lead us.

Silence

You speak what is true:
and the truth can set us free.

Heavenly Father, give to all leaders
and their advisers
the courage to be honest,
the will to be just,
the greatness to be humble
and the openness to learn.

Silence

You speak what is true:
and the truth can set us free.

Heavenly Father, at the door of each home
place your welcome;
in the rooms of each home, your love;
in the eyes of each person, your truth;
and in all our companionship, your own.

Silence

You speak what is true:
and the truth can set us free.

Heavenly Father, give comfort and healing
to those who are ill,
peace to the anxious,
and reassurance to the afraid;
may we know your love for us
through both the good and the agonising times.

Silence

You speak what is true:
and the truth can set us free.

Heavenly Father, may the dying be prepared
to meet you,
and the souls of those who have died in faith
live for ever in the joy of your presence.

Silence

You speak what is true:
and the truth can set us free.

Heavenly Father, give us thankful hearts
to bless your name in sadness and in joy,
knowing that you are always there beside us.

Merciful Father,
accept these prayers
for the sake of your Son,
our Saviour Jesus Christ. Amen.

THIRD SUNDAY
OF LENT

God's wisdom may shock us. Jesus, obedient to
God's Law and fulfilling it, dies a death which,
according to the Law, makes him cursed.

As God has called us,
so we have come to pray.

We pray for the Church, the Body of Christ,
with all its collected gifts and weaknesses;
give us the grace to recognise
that in your Spirit we are one,
and curb in us all tendency to division.

Silence

May we hear you, Lord:
and want to obey.

We pray for the world
in all its beauty and richness;
give us the desire
to share our planet's food and resources,
to care for its people's well-being,
and to foster peace and justice for all.

Silence

May we hear you, Lord:
and want to obey.

We pray for those we love –
those we see each day and those we miss;
help us to cherish one another
as we live the loving way of your commands.

Silence

May we hear you, Lord:
and want to obey.

We pray for all victims of selfish or violent acts,
and for those whose lives are trapped in sin.
We pray for all whose bodies and minds
have difficulty functioning.
Make us more sensitive to their needs.

Silence

May we hear you, Lord:
and want to obey.

We pray for those who have died
and for those who miss their physical presence.
Have mercy on them;
may they, and we in our turn,
rest in the peace of your enfolding.

Silence

May we hear you, Lord:
and want to obey.

We give you thanks
for the loving example of Jesus,
who was obedient even to death
and strengthens us in all goodness.

Merciful Father,
**accept these prayers
for the sake of your Son,
our Saviour Jesus Christ. Amen.**

FOURTH SUNDAY OF LENT
MOTHERING SUNDAY

*God provides comfort in all
our troubles and sufferings.*

As we gather together
in the presence of our parent God,
let us pray.

Loving Father, we pray
for all who are persecuted for their faith,
and for whom following you brings danger.
We pray for those who are new to faith
and those who no longer walk with you.
We thank you for the example of those
whose faith shines out in their lives.

Silence

We are all your children:
help us grow in love.

Loving Father, we pray
for those who are forced to leave their homes,
their families or their countries.
We pray for those who, through war and famine,
must watch their children die.
We pray for your peace and comfort.

Silence

We are all your children:
help us grow in love.

Loving Father, we pray
for all the mothering that goes on in this community
and for those who crave tenderness
and are weary of the struggle to be strong.

Silence

We are all your children:
help us grow in love.

Loving Father, we pray
for all new parents and their babies,
and all giving birth today.
We pray for all who are vulnerable,
that they may be protected from harm.

Silence

We are all your children:
help us grow in love.

Loving Father, there are those here
whose mothers have died,
and are still remembered with great affection.
We pray for those mothers and grandmothers now,
rejoicing in all they gave,
and commending them to your protection for ever.

Silence

We are all your children:
help us grow in love.

Loving Father, we give you thanks
for the comfort you provide in all our troubles,
and for the richness of all our relationships.

Merciful Father,
**accept these prayers
for the sake of your Son,
our Saviour Jesus Christ. Amen.**

FIFTH SUNDAY OF LENT

*Through Christ's death, full life would come
to people of all nations and generations.*

Let us pray to the God who loves us
and understands our needs.

God of mercy, we pray for all Church leaders,
teachers and pastors,
and all who are being called
into particular ministries, both lay and ordained.
We pray especially for any who are wrestling
with the demands of such a calling,
that they may be given courage
to offer themselves in your service.

Silence

Let your name be glorified:
let your will be done.

All-seeing God, watch over the nations of the world
in all their plans and actions, conflicts and disasters;
guard the children, guide the leaders
and give us all your peace.

Silence

Let your name be glorified:
let your will be done.

God of love, be present in every heart and home,
to cherish, to challenge,
to reassure and to comfort us.

Silence

Let your name be glorified:
let your will be done.

God of wholeness, we bring to your love
those who are weighed down with suffering,
or imprisoned by their fears.
Ease their burdens and give them the strength
to bear what cannot be avoided.

Silence

Let your name be glorified:
let your will be done.

God of life, we bring to you those
whose earthly lives have ended,
that in your mercy they may have everlasting peace.

Silence

Let your name be glorified:
let your will be done.

Gracious God, you are always
so much more ready to give than we to receive;
open our hearts and minds
to live the costly way of love.

Merciful Father,
**accept these prayers
for the sake of your Son,
our Saviour Jesus Christ. Amen.**

PALM SUNDAY

As the Messiah, Jesus enters Jerusalem,
knowing that he rides towards rejection
and death in order to save his people.

As we face up to the costly loving
shown by our God,
let us approach him in humility
and pray to him now.

O God, give us in your Church undivided hearts
to love you and one another, and go on loving,
through insult and praise,
through acceptance and rejection,
in the sure knowledge that you are Lord.

Silence

Make us strong:
to do your will in all things.

O God, may the kingdoms of this world
soak up the values of your kingdom;
may their leaders and their peoples
uphold what is right and just,
and establish a social order
which is rooted in Godly love.

Silence

Make us strong:
to do your will in all things.

O God, in all the heartaches and joys
of human relationships,
may we be governed by selfless love,
faithful and forgiving like you,
without limit.

Silence

Make us strong:
to do your will in all things.

O God, draw alongside all who suffer
that they may know the comfort of your presence
and the healing power of your forgiving love.

Silence

Make us strong:
to do your will in all things.

O God, we pray for all
who are making that last journey of death,
that they may be surrounded with your peace
and rest in your love for ever.

Silence

Make us strong:
to do your will in all things.

O God, we give you thanks
that the Messiah has come to save your people.

Merciful Father,
accept these prayers
for the sake of your Son,
our Saviour Jesus Christ. Amen.

EASTER DAY

Jesus is alive; Love has won the
victory over sin and death.

As we celebrate the risen Christ,
let us pray to the God of life,
in whom we live.

That the Church of God
may be bursting with new life,
filled with the love
that takes even death in its stride;
that new and mature Christians together,
all in their various ministries,
may work in God's strength
for the coming kingdom.

Silence

You are our God:
who does all things well.

That the inhabitants of our planet
may recognise God's glory all around,
co-operate in the sharing of his gifts,
and cultivate the habit of caring love.

Silence

You are our God:
who does all things well.

That God will bless our homes and families,
our places of work and leisure,
with new life and the hope of new possibilities
touching the ordinary with beauty and joy.

Silence

You are our God:
who does all things well.

That all who feel trapped or imprisoned –
physically, mentally or spiritually –
may feel the stones rolled away
and new light pouring into their lives.

Silence

You are our God:
who does all things well.

That those who have died to this earthly life
may find the fullness of God's eternity,
flooded with the light of his love.

Silence

You are our God:
who does all things well.

That we may live each moment thankfully,
assured of God's company and mercy.

Merciful Father,
accept these prayers
for the sake of your Son,
our Saviour Jesus Christ. Amen.

SECOND SUNDAY OF EASTER

*Our faith in the risen Christ
is bound to affect the way we live.*

Knowing that the risen Christ is here among us,
let us pray in his name
for the Church and for the world.

Father, we pray for your blessing
on every group of Christians worshipping today
all over the world;
and we pray for all who doubt your truth.
We pray that our hearts may be set ablaze
with love,
and that we may walk as children of light.

Silence

My Lord and my God!
My Lord and my God!

Father, we pray for all the areas of your world
which are torn apart by hatred and violence,
famine, disease, or religious differences;
we pray for an end to war
and a deeper commitment to peace.

Silence

My Lord and my God!
My Lord and my God!

Father, we pray for those who face family rejection
if they become Christians,
and for all families divided by beliefs
or persecuted for their faith.
We pray for the children of our church
that they may grow up strong in the faith
with good role models to guide them.

Silence

My Lord and my God!
My Lord and my God!

Father, we pray for those who wake up
to the prospect of another day filled with pain;
for those who long for someone
to spend time with them, enjoying their company;
and we pray for sight that notices needs.

Silence

My Lord and my God!
My Lord and my God!

Father, we pray for those who mourn,
and we pray for those they love and miss,
commending all who have died
to the everlasting arms of the God of love,
in whom there is life in all its fullness.

Silence

My Lord and my God!
My Lord and my God!

Father, with joy in our hearts we thank you
for the new life opened up to us
through Jesus, our Redeemer.

Merciful Father,
accept these prayers
for the sake of your Son,
our Saviour Jesus Christ. Amen.

THIRD SUNDAY OF EASTER

Having redeemed us by his death, Jesus can offer us
the forgiveness of our sin, which sets us free to live.

May God be glorified now,
as we commit ourselves to the work of prayer,
interceding for those in all kinds of need.

In our worship,
and our openness to the Spirit of life,
in the Church's longing and outreach,
in the priests, the people,
in all seekers and honest doubters,

in all this:
may God be glorified.

Silence

In the welfare programmes
and peace-making missions,
in the struggle to uphold justice,
in the aid given to the hungry and homeless,

in all this:
may God be glorified.

Silence

In the loving and costly commitment
of mothers and fathers, brothers and sisters,
daughters and sons,
in the determination to forgive and forgive,
in all the lives shared and cherished,

in all this:
may God be glorified.

Silence

In the work of nursing, comforting and healing,
in the daily patient struggle
with pain and weakness,
and in the practical, good-humoured caring,

in all this:
may God be glorified.

Silence

In the twilight years and the facing of death,
in lives well lived and now breaking into eternity,

in all this:
may God be glorified.

Silence

In the freedom offered through forgiveness,
in the joy of Resurrection life,
in the hope of eternity,

in all this:
may God be glorified.

Silence

Merciful Father,
accept these prayers
for the sake of your Son,
our Saviour Jesus Christ. Amen.

FOURTH SUNDAY OF EASTER

*'I am the Good Shepherd
and I lay down my life for the sheep.'*

The Lord is our Shepherd;
knowing his care for us, let us pray.

For all who shepherd others
as bishops and pastors,
and for all in their care;
for Christians threatened and under attack;
and all whose ministry feels demanding.
For a greater affection and care,
one for another, in the Church.

Silence

The Lord is our Good Shepherd:
there is nothing we shall lack.

We pray for all in positions of leadership
and influence in our world,
that they may use that power for good;
for an increase in our concern
for one another's well-being, across all barriers,
and for all who are working to build community.

Silence

The Lord is our Good Shepherd:
there is nothing we shall lack.

We pray for those who are wandering, lost and aimless,
with no idea that any Good Shepherd exists;
for those who die unaware that they are precious
and valued by the God who loved them into being.

Silence

The Lord is our Good Shepherd:
there is nothing we shall lack.

We pray for those who have died
to this earthly life,
that the Good Shepherd,
who understands what it is to die,
may bring them safely home.

Silence

The Lord is our Good Shepherd:
there is nothing we shall lack.

We pray in thankfulness
for your shepherding of us,
and own you as our Good Shepherd
in whom we are kept safe for ever.

Merciful Father,
accept these prayers
for the sake of your Son,
our Saviour Jesus Christ. Amen.

FIFTH SUNDAY OF EASTER

*To produce fruit we need to be
joined on to the true vine.*

Let us pray to the Lord God Almighty,
in whom we live and move and have our being.

Father, we want to produce good fruit in abundance;
nurture us as branches of the true vine,
train and prune us where necessary,
and may our spiritual harvest make rich wine,
wine of your kingdom.

Silence

Your kingdom, let it come!
Your will, let it be done!

Father, clearly we see around our world
the tragic and expensive consequences
of branches cut off from the true vine.
We pray for a seeking after your truth
and a desire to act rightly and justly
in all areas of human society.

Silence

Your kingdom, let it come!
Your will, let it be done!

Father, we pray for those to whom we are linked
by family, friendships or work;
especially we pray for those
separated from their loved ones or their home.

Silence

Your kingdom, let it come!
Your will, let it be done!

Father, we long for healing and wholeness
in all who suffer
and in all dysfunctional communities;
guide us to understand
how we might be part of the healing.

Silence

Your kingdom, let it come!
Your will, let it be done!

Father, we know that death
cannot separate us from your love;
in that knowledge we commend to your keeping
those who have died and all who miss them.

Silence

Your kingdom, let it come!
Your will, let it be done!

Father, we thank you that we can live
in the joyful freedom of your love,
as we dedicate ourselves to serving others.

Merciful Father,
**accept these prayers
for the sake of your Son,
our Saviour Jesus Christ. Amen.**

SIXTH SUNDAY OF EASTER

We are to love one another as Jesus loves us.

Knowing God's love and affection for us,
let us pray to him now.

Father, wherever there is friction and conflict
in the Church,
and communities are divided and weakened;
give us a greater longing for your healing
and a deeper commitment to forgiving love.

Silence

Help us, Lord:
to love one another.

Father, wherever tangled political situations
seem impossible to solve,
wherever conflicting interests threaten peace;
wherever the ears of the powerful
remain insulated against the cries of the oppressed;
give us ears to hear your guidance.

Silence

Help us, Lord:
to love one another.

Father, wherever families are dysfunctional
or children are in danger;
wherever the daily living conditions
are damaging to health and self-respect;
let your kingdom come.

Silence

Help us, Lord:
to love one another.

Father, wherever the ill and injured
need comfort and assistance;
wherever the elderly and housebound
sit each day for hours alone;
may we bring your love and help.

Silence

Help us, Lord:
to love one another.

Father, wherever people are travelling
that last journey of death,
may they be surrounded by your love
and welcomed into your heaven,
and may those who mourn be comforted.

Silence

Help us, Lord:
to love one another.

Father, wherever the beauty of creation
reflects your love,
may our hearts be lifted to you
in thanks and praise.

Merciful Father,
accept these prayers
for the sake of your Son,
our Saviour Jesus Christ. Amen.

ASCENSION DAY

Having bought back our freedom with the giving of his life,
Jesus enters into the full glory to which he is entitled.

Rejoicing that Jesus has ascended into the heavens,
let us pray in confidence to God our Father.

We pray in thankfulness
for those who introduced us to Jesus
and who help us along our spiritual journey.
We pray for one another in this church
and for all Christians, young and old,
throughout the world.

Silence

Let the kingdom come:
let your kingdom come.

We pray with longing
for the world to be governed
in accordance with your law of love;
that all your creation may be reverenced
and treated with respect.

Silence

Let the kingdom come:
let your kingdom come.

We pray with concern
for all the homes, schools and places of work
in this community;
rejoicing in all that is of you,
and asking your healing forgiveness
wherever there is discord or bitterness.

Silence

Let the kingdom come:
let your kingdom come.

We pray with hope
for the healing and restoration to wholeness
of all who are ill or troubled,
damaged or depressed.

Silence

Let the kingdom come:
let your kingdom come.

We pray with confidence
for those who have come to the end
of their earthly lives,
that they may be given merciful judgement
and welcomed into the glory of heaven.

Silence

Let the kingdom come:
let your kingdom come.

We pray with joy
as we celebrate Jesus entering the glory
he so richly deserves, and look expectantly
towards his second coming.

Merciful Father,
accept these prayers
for the sake of your Son,
our Saviour Jesus Christ. Amen.

SEVENTH SUNDAY OF EASTER

Although now hidden from our sight,
Jesus lives for ever, and in him we can live
the Resurrection life even while we are on earth.

Let us pray together to our heavenly Father,
knowing his love for us.

Father, we want to live your way
and do your will,
offer you true worship,
and serve one another in love.
Empower your Church to do this, we pray;
live in us; transform us.

Silence

Lord, we wait on you:
fill us, Holy Spirit of God.

Father, we want our states and kingdoms
to display your love and truth, justice and mercy.
We want to break down walls of prejudice
and build bridges of reconciliation and trust.
Empower your world, we pray;
live in us; transform us.

Silence

Lord, we wait on you:
fill us, Holy Spirit of God.

Father, we want our children
to be safely and lovingly nurtured,
our elderly valued,
our homes to be places of welcome and warmth;
empower your people, we pray:
live in us; transform us.

Silence

Lord, we wait on you:
fill us, Holy Spirit of God.

Father, we want your healing
for those whose lives are aching and weary;
your comfort and reassurance
for all who are imprisoned by fears and hate;
empower these lives, we pray;
live in us; transform us.

Silence

Lord, we wait on you:
fill us, Holy Spirit of God.

Father, we want to commit our loved ones,
who have died, into your safe keeping for ever.
Prepare us all, Father, to live with you in heaven.

Silence

Lord, we wait on you:
fill us, Holy Spirit of God.

Father, we want to worship and praise you
with our voices and our lives;
shape us to your purpose, and use us.

Merciful Father,
**accept these prayers
for the sake of your Son,
our Saviour Jesus Christ. Amen.**

PENTECOST

*The Holy Spirit of God is poured out in power on the
expectant disciples, just as Jesus promised.*

In the power of the Holy Spirit,
let us pray.

For a fresh in-breathing of life and power
in each church community,
which breaks down our barriers
and sets us on fire with God's love.

Silence

Come, Holy Spirit:
Holy Spirit, come!

For the grace to see this world
and its needs and problems
through the eyes of love, hope,
justice and mercy;
for the grace to abandon prejudice
and build bridges of reconciliation.

Silence

Come, Holy Spirit:
Holy Spirit, come!

For the Spirit of loving kindness
to fill our homes, schools and places of work;
for family rifts to be healed
and long-standing conflicts resolved.

Silence

Come, Holy Spirit:
Holy Spirit, come!

For the restoration of those who are sick
to wholeness and well-being;
for courage and patience in all suffering,
and for good to be distilled
from every painful, destructive experience.

Silence

Come, Holy Spirit:
Holy Spirit, come!

For God's merciful judgement
on those who have died,
and the opportunity for us all
to prepare carefully for meeting God
face to face.

Silence

Come, Holy Spirit:
Holy Spirit, come!

For a deeper knowledge and love
of the God who knows and loves us completely.

Merciful Father,
accept these prayers
for the sake of your Son,
our Saviour Jesus Christ. Amen.

TRINITY SUNDAY

*The mysterious and holy nature of the one true
God is beyond our understanding, but it is
both communal harmony and individual
personality, Father, Son and Holy Spirit.*

Let us pray to the Father
through the Son
and in the power of the Holy Spirit.

Lord God, may the Church reflect
your community and unity;
may there be Godly harmony, shared ministry,
mutual support and encouragement in the faith.

Silence

May your will be done:
on earth as it is in heaven.

Lord God, may the world's leaders
seek not personal power but the public good;
may conflicts be faced honestly
and needs recognised and met;
may all our communities be built up
on what is good, true, just and right.

Silence

May your will be done:
on earth as it is in heaven.

Lord God, may there be love and respect
for one another in every household;
may there be mutual support
and thoughtfulness, consideration and trust.

Silence

May your will be done:
on earth as it is in heaven.

Lord God, may the hearts' cries for help be heard;
the tears collected and the fears quieted;
may suffering be eased and guilt erased
through your healing love.

Silence

May your will be done:
on earth as it is in heaven.

Lord God, may the dead rise
to new and eternal life,
freed from their aching and restored for ever.

Silence

May your will be done:
on earth as it is in heaven.

Lord God, we pour out to you
our praise and wonder
at the hidden mysterious holiness
of your Being, so full of glory and love!

Merciful Father,
accept these prayers
for the sake of your Son,
our Saviour Jesus Christ. Amen.

PROPER 4

Sunday between 29 May and 4 June inclusive
(if after Trinity Sunday)

Jesus has the words of eternal life – he sheds
light on a right attitude to the Law.

Through Jesus
we are shown God's compassion and mercy;
let us pray for that love in our lives,
in the Church and in the world.

Let compassion and mercy
be the hallmarks of our church life
and all its activities;
let us be noticeable by their shining
in our behaviour and our conversations;
disrupt any rules which block them out.

Silence

Lord of love:
let only your will be done.

Let compassion and mercy
take root in every institution, policy and structure;
let them challenge accepted wrongs
and disturb complacency.

Silence

Lord of love:
let only your will be done.

Let compassion and mercy
guard every doorway and fill every room;
let them colour each encounter
and drive every decision.

Silence

Lord of love:
let only your will be done.

Let compassion and mercy
transform our attitudes
to all whose illness or frailty
makes them marginalised, ignored or despised.
Let there be healing of all damaged self-perception,
and restoration of jarred human dignity.

Silence

Lord of love:
let only your will be done.

Let compassion and mercy
accompany the dying
and welcome them into eternity.

Silence

Lord of love:
let only your will be done.

Let compassion and mercy
blossom in all of us,
as we live out our thankfulness
to the God of love,
for all his goodness to us.

Merciful Father,
accept these prayers
for the sake of your Son,
our Saviour Jesus Christ. Amen.

PROPER 5

Sunday between 5 and 11 June inclusive
(if after Trinity Sunday)

Anyone who does God's will is considered
a close family member of Jesus.

As members of God's family,
let us pray together to our heavenly Father.

That as family members of the Church of God
we may show his likeness by doing his will;
that those visiting our churches
may find there God's beauty and truth,
open-hearted loving and a unity of purpose.

Silence

Father:
let your will be done.

That as members of the human race
we may work together, share resources,
respect and learn from one another.
That leaders may inspire collective good,
and those with vision be valued and heard.

Silence

Father:
let your will be done.

That we may give both support and space
to those we love and nurture;
that those of our own families
who do not yet know God
may come to understand the depth
of his love for them.

Silence

Father:
let your will be done.

That all who come to Jesus in need
may find in him forgiveness, healing
and wholeness of body, mind and spirit,
strength to cope with their difficulties
and a constant inner renewing.

Silence

Father:
let your will be done.

That as those coming to death
roll up the tents of their earthly existence,
they may be welcomed into the eternal home
prepared for them by their loving God.

Silence

Father:
let your will be done.

That as we marvel at the generosity
of God's love, and his acceptance of us,
we may grow closer to his likeness
each day we live.

Merciful Father,
accept these prayers
for the sake of your Son,
our Saviour Jesus Christ. Amen.

PROPER 6

Sunday between 12 and 18 June inclusive
(if after Trinity Sunday)

From small beginnings, and by God's power,
the kingdom of heaven grows.

Let us pray to the God of heaven and earth
for the growth of the kingdom.

May the kingdom grow
in clusters of Christians all over the world;
may it grow as hearts are warmed
by encounter with the living God;
nourished by word and sacrament,
private prayer and public worship.

Silence

Lord of heaven:
let the kingdom grow!

May the kingdom grow
in states, empires and monarchies,
in the crowded streets of cities
and in the scattered rural communities;
in all decision-making and all spending.

Silence

Lord of heaven:
let the kingdom grow!

May the kingdom grow
in every human shelter and home,
every place of work and education,
in each conversation and
in our mutual care of one another.

Silence

Lord of heaven:
let the kingdom grow!

May the kingdom grow
to bring peace and healing
wherever there is pain or sadness;
to bring reassurance, comfort, courage and hope.

Silence

Lord of heaven:
let the kingdom grow!

In the knowledge that we must all face judgement,
we pray for those who have died,
thanking God for his loving mercy,
and entrusting our loved ones
to God's safe keeping.

Silence

Lord of heaven:
let the kingdom grow!

As we thank God for all his blessings to us
we offer him the rest of our lives.

Merciful Father,
accept these prayers
for the sake of your Son,
our Saviour Jesus Christ. Amen.

PROPER 7

Sunday between 19 and 25 June inclusive
(if after Trinity Sunday)

What kind of person is this?
Even the wind and waves obey him.

As residents of God's universe,
let us pray now to our loving Creator.

Lord of all truth and goodness,
we pray for those in positions of authority
in the Church all over the world
and in each gathered community;
that in all the storms
we may be enabled to hear God's calming voice
and deepen our trust in him.

Silence

Calm our fears:
and teach us your peace.

Lord of great power and majesty,
we pray for those with political and military power,
and all whose decisions affect many lives.
Speak truth into motives, honour into actions
and your vision of peace into every conflict.

Silence

Calm our fears:
and teach us your peace.

Heavenly Father, we pray for all single people,
couples, communal groups and families,
as they weather their storms and learn from them;
lavish on all who have the care of others
the capacity to bring peace and calm fears.

Silence

Calm our fears:
and teach us your peace.

Lord of all healing, we pray for those
whose minds and hearts are in turmoil,
whose lives lurch from crisis to crisis;
for those who find their lives shattered
by illness or injury;
for peace in those threatening storms
and a settling of all anxiety.

Silence

Calm our fears:
and teach us your peace.

Lord of eternity, we thank you
for your reassurance of life beyond physical death;
we pray for those who are dying alone,
unnoticed or unprepared;
we commend those who have died
to God's merciful forgiveness and eternal tranquillity.

Silence

Calm our fears:
and teach us your peace.

Lord of creation,
we are full of wonder at the story of your universe,
spoken into existence and sustained with such love.

Merciful Father,
accept these prayers
for the sake of your Son,
our Saviour Jesus Christ. Amen.

PROPER 8

Sunday between 26 June and 2 July inclusive

God's power can reach even into death and draw out life.

As God has called us by name
out into full, abundant life,
let us lay before him now our concerns
for the Church and for the world.

Father, chip away from your Church
all the built-up layers
of complacency or despondency,
of over-comfortable familiarity
or under-active expectation,
until we see again
with the freshness and wonder of deepened faith.

Silence

Lord, we believe:
help our unbelief.

Father, we call to mind
societies and systems of our world.
Question our assumptions
and challenge our destructive choices;
break away the unnoticed scales of prejudice
which blind us,
so that our world may become
increasingly under your reign of justice,
righteousness and love.

Silence

Lord, we believe:
help our unbelief.

Father, replace our pride with humility
until we learn from young children

the lessons of wonder and trust.
Keep the childlike as a living flame
in all of us, whatever our age,
and enable us to rediscover your glory all around us.

Silence

Lord, we believe:
help our unbelief.

Father, as the sick were brought to Jesus
by their loved ones,
so we bring to you now all those
whom we long to be healed.
May they hear your voice and sense your touch.

Silence

Lord, we believe:
help our unbelief.

Father, earth-bound we grieve
at the loss of loved ones through death;
yet we also rejoice in you calling them out
into the fullness of everlasting life.

Silence

Lord, we believe:
help our unbelief.

Father, we thank you for the amazing truth
that you always reach out to us in compassion,
and always have time for us.

Merciful Father,
accept these prayers
for the sake of your Son,
our Saviour Jesus Christ. Amen.

PROPER 9

Sunday between 3 and 9 July inclusive

If we are not ready to listen to the truth,
we will not hear it.

God has drawn us down many different routes
to this shared worship today.
Let us still our bodies
and alert our minds and hearts in his presence.

Heavenly Father, we are only the Body of Christ
because your Spirit binds us together with your life.
Give us real concern and love for one another,
supportive and encouraging,
without malice or bickering,
so that we can be sent out
strong in our weakness and littleness.

Silence

Give us your grace:
to hear your word with joy.

Heavenly Father, all the kingdoms and states
are answerable to your authority,
and much evil is allowed to flourish
through the silence of good people;
give us all the courage to speak out your truth,
whether it is popular or not.

Silence

Give us your grace:
to hear your word with joy.

Heavenly Father, be in all our listening
at home, on the phone, at school and at work;
may we give our full attention to you
and to one another,
happy to grow wiser through each conversation.

Silence

Give us your grace:
to hear your word with joy.

Heavenly Father, we pray for those
whose pain screams silently and incessantly;
for those who have no one to confide in,
no one to listen.
We pray for your love to enfold them,
your peace to calm them
and your healing to transform them.

Silence

Give us your grace:
to hear your word with joy.

Heavenly Father, prepare us all during this life
for the life to come;
we commend to your keeping all those
who have recently made their journey through death.

Silence

Give us your grace:
to hear your word with joy.

Heavenly Father, we thank you
for making your ways known to us
and guiding us into your truth.

Merciful Father,
accept these prayers
for the sake of your Son,
our Saviour Jesus Christ. Amen.

PROPER 10

Sunday between 10 and 16 July inclusive

*Those who speak out God's will are bound
to be vulnerable to rejection and abuse.*

In humility and love
let us draw near to our God
and pray to him now.

Lord God, we pray that our lives
may be upright and holy;
that our church communities may shine
with goodness and love, humility and truth;
we pray for all leaning lives to be straightened up
through your merciful forgiveness.

Silence

Holy God, scatter all darkness:
and bathe our world in your light.

Lord God, we pray that many
may be empowered to recognise evil
and fight against it;
to discern your warnings and speak them out;
to notice the sparks of love and goodness
and celebrate them.

Silence

Holy God, scatter all darkness:
and bathe our world in your light.

Lord God, we pray that our households
and neighbourhoods,
our places of work and leisure,
may be arenas of praise and thankfulness,
not only in the comfort zones
but particularly through the disturbed
and difficult times.

Silence

Holy God, scatter all darkness:
and bathe our world in your light.

Lord God, we pray for those in prison;
for those leading cruel and violent lives;
for all victims of oppression or abuse;
for all who suffer mental anguish or physical pain.

Silence

Holy God, scatter all darkness:
and bathe our world in your light.

Lord God, we pray for those who have died,
that they, and we in our turn, may be given
merciful judgement through Jesus our Saviour,
and brought into the unquenchable light of heaven.

Silence

Holy God, scatter all darkness:
and bathe our world in your light.

Lord God, we pray for more thankful hearts
to bless you, because the gifts we receive from you
are so much more than we deserve.

Merciful Father,
accept these prayers
for the sake of your Son,
our Saviour Jesus Christ. Amen.

PROPER 11
Sunday between 17 and 23 July inclusive

Like a good shepherd, Jesus sees the needs
of his people and always responds with love.

Knowing God's love and concern for us all,
let us settle ourselves in his presence
and pray to him now.

Recognising our brokenness and disunity
as your Church,
we pray for your leading
to draw us closer to one another
as we draw closer to you;
we pray for all our Christian brothers and sisters
in this neighbourhood,
and for all who are searching for meaning in their lives.

Silence

The Lord is my shepherd:
there is nothing I shall want.

With the noise of global conflicts
and human deprivation thundering in our ears,
with the questions and doubts clamouring,
we pray for your shepherding of our humanness
and your leading in the secret places of the heart.

Silence

The Lord is my shepherd:
there is nothing I shall want.

With the statistics of family life
challenging our values,
and with the pressures to conform to norms
in conflict with God's will,
we pray for your sound and centred wisdom
in all our daily living and life choices.

Silence

The Lord is my shepherd:
there is nothing I shall want.

With the stressed and overburdened,
the overworked and the unemployed,
we pray for balanced lives;
for physical, mental and spiritual health;
for patience in times of trouble,
and direction in times of confusion.

Silence

The Lord is my shepherd:
there is nothing I shall want.

As we remember with love and gratitude
the lives of those who have died in faith,
we commend them to your eternal rest
and unchanging affection.

Silence

The Lord is my shepherd:
there is nothing I shall want.

With the crowds of Galilee
our hearts are lifted with joy at your presence among us,
for we know that you have the words of eternal life.

Merciful Father,
accept these prayers
for the sake of your Son,
our Saviour Jesus Christ. Amen.

PROPER 12

Sunday between 24 and 30 July inclusive

*Out of God's riches, a great crowd is fed and satisfied
from a small offering of food.*

Knowing that our loving God
supplies all our needs,
let us pray to him now
on behalf of the Church and the world.

Father, we offer this time and the love of our hearts
as we pray for the Church with all its varied ministries;
for the youngest to the oldest baptised members;
for those of mellow faith
and those who struggle with doubts.

Silence

Loving Father:
give us today our daily bread.

Father, we offer our commitment
to pray the news each day
and share the pain we read about,
longing for your peace and your justice
in a world tense with aggression
and distorted with selfishness.

Silence

Loving Father:
give us today our daily bread.

Father, we offer our homes and our relationships
for you to work in and transform;
we offer you our meetings and conflicts
and all differences of opinion
for you to use to your glory.

Silence

Loving Father:
give us today our daily bread.

Father, we offer you our solidarity
with all who suffer or are heavily burdened;
hear us as we pray
for their comfort and refreshment,
wholeness and restoration,
but above all for the consciousness
of your presence in their pain,
and your love for them.

Silence

Loving Father:
give us today our daily bread.

Father, we offer our thanks for lives well lived
and faithful souls entering by the gate
of physical death to eternal life with you.
Prepare us all to meet you face to face.

Silence

Loving Father:
give us today our daily bread.

Father, we give you our lives
as well as our words of praise,
so that each moment from now on
becomes an offering of love.

Merciful Father,
accept these prayers
for the sake of your Son,
our Saviour Jesus Christ. Amen.

PROPER 13

Sunday between 31 July and 6 August inclusive

*Jesus is the Bread of Life who satisfies our hunger
and sustains us on our journey to heaven.*

Let us pray to the God who loves us,
knows our needs, and provides for us.

As the travelling people of God,
we pray for a deepening hunger
for the things of God
and a loosening of our grip
on all the wants and expectations
which prevent us from moving forward God's way.

Silence

Feed us, Father:
with the Bread of Life.

As brothers and sisters with the whole of creation,
we pray for respect and reverence among people
regardless of wealth or status;
for responsible sharing of resources
and consideration for the natural world
of our fragile and beautiful planet.

Silence

Feed us, Father:
with the Bread of Life.

As we prepare and eat our food each day,
we pray for those who grow and manufacture it,
distribute and sell it, shop for it and cook it,
and for those with whom we share food.
Build us up with your spiritual feeding
which sustains us for ever.

Silence

Feed us, Father:
with the Bread of Life.

As we ask for daily bread,
we pray for those who are physically starving,
for all who hunger emotionally
or try to survive on spiritual junk food;
for those who mistrust God's feeding.

Silence

Feed us, Father:
with the Bread of Life.

As we remember with love
those who have journeyed through physical death,
we pray that, nourished by the Bread of Life,
they may travel on eagles' wings
into the brightness of eternal life.

Silence

Feed us, Father:
with the Bread of Life.

As we grow increasingly aware
of our spiritual hunger,
we give thanks for the wonder of God's feeding,
throughout our days.

Merciful Father,
accept these prayers
for the sake of your Son,
our Saviour Jesus Christ. Amen.

PROPER 14

Sunday between 7 and 13 August inclusive

*Just as bread is the visible form of life-giving
nourishment, so Jesus is the visible form
of God's life-giving love.*

Let us pray to our God
as we worship him in Spirit and in truth.

Heavenly Father, we pray for all
who are commissioned and called
to work as leaders and prophets in your Church.
We pray for greater discernment of your presence
and your will in our Christian communities,
and a clearing away of all that obscures our vision.

Silence

Open our eyes:
to see your glory.

Heavenly Father, we pray against the cynicism
and complacency that deaden wonder.
In the ordinary things of life
may we detect your love and wisdom;
through the everyday events
may we encounter you, walking alongside us.

Silence

Open our eyes:
to see your glory.

Heavenly Father, we pray for breadwinners
and sandwich makers, and all food growers;
for your presence in kitchens, dining rooms,
canteens, restaurants and bars;
wherever people gather to eat together,
may they find you there with them.

Silence

Open our eyes:
to see your glory.

Heavenly Father, we pray for those
whose emotional damage makes trusting and receiving
seem threatening and dangerous.
We pray for peace of mind for the anxious,
and hope for all who are close to despair.

Silence

Open our eyes:
to see your glory.

Heavenly Father, we pray for those
who have reached the boundary of death,
that in faith they may journey through it
and out into the unconfined space and joy of heaven.

Silence

Open our eyes:
to see your glory.

Heavenly Father, we rejoice
that the ordinary things of this world
are saturated with your extraordinary love.

Merciful Father,
accept these prayers
for the sake of your Son,
our Saviour Jesus Christ. Amen.

PROPER 15

Sunday between 14 and 20 August inclusive

*God's wisdom may appear foolishness without
the God-given grace to understand.*

As we gather, conscious of our need of wisdom,
let us pray to our wise and loving God.

Father, in all the decision-making,
problems and challenges of our church,
we ask your counsel and encouragement;
in all our worship and outreach,
we invite you to lead us.

Silence

Wise and loving God:
quieten us to hear your voice.

Father, in all the clashes of needs and wants,
the half-forgotten hurts that drive aggression,
the half-remembered grievances,
barbed with revenge,
in all the world's raging and protesting,
sink your spirit of peace and reconciliation.

Silence

Wise and loving God:
quieten us to hear your voice.

Father, in the daily batch of misunderstandings,
conflicting loyalties, negotiations and compromise,
walk among us in our homes and places of work,
whispering sanity and mutual respect.

Silence

Wise and loving God:
quieten us to hear your voice.

Father, in those engulfed by pain
or enslaved by addiction,
bring hope and healing;
bless all those whose minds think simply
and rely on others for basic care.

Silence

Wise and loving God:
quieten us to hear your voice.

Father, gather into your keeping for ever
all who have left this life in your friendship;
we pray too for those approaching death,
that they may know your love
surrounding them across time and eternity.

Silence

Wise and loving God:
quieten us to hear your voice.

Father, in all our wondering and wandering,
we thank you for your patience with us
and your understanding of our journey.

Merciful Father,
**accept these prayers
for the sake of your Son,
our Saviour Jesus Christ. Amen.**

PROPER 16

Sunday between 21 and 27 August inclusive

'To whom else could we go?
You alone have the words of eternal life.'

We have chosen to serve the Lord.
Let us pray to him now.

We pray for those whose faith
is being challenged or undermined
by inner doubts or outside influences.
We pray for those who build up our faith
and all who strive to proclaim the Gospel
in language that people understand.

Silence

Holy God, we believe:
help our unbelief.

We pray for our torn and fragmented world,
wrestling to equate the deep yearning for peace
with the instinctive urge for gratification and power;
that many may have the courage to walk God's way.

Silence

Holy God, we believe:
help our unbelief.

We pray for our loved ones;
for those who lift our hearts
and those who turn our hair grey.
We pray for those we instinctively warm to
and those with whom
there are frequent misunderstandings.
We thank God for our opportunities of forgiveness.

Silence

Holy God, we believe:
help our unbelief.

We pray for all who are marginalised,
scorned or rejected;
for those isolated through illness or imprisonment;
for those who feel that no one understands.
Surround them all with such love
that they may know they are precious to you.

Silence

Holy God, we believe:
help our unbelief.

We pray for those approaching death,
that through our prayers they may know themselves
accompanied with love on that journey.
We pray for those who have died,
that they may come to know the full joy of heaven.

Silence

Holy God, we believe:
help our unbelief.

We thank you, Holy God,
for making yourself known to us,
both in daily living
and sacramentally in the breaking of bread.

Merciful Father,
accept these prayers
for the sake of your Son,
our Saviour Jesus Christ. Amen.

PROPER 17

Sunday between 28 August and 3 September inclusive

*We need to be careful never to replace the timeless
commands of God with man-made traditions.*

Our God is the source of all holiness;
with the needs of the Church and the world
close to our hearts,
let us pray to the only one
who can renew and redeem.

Father, we are all too aware of our temptation
to place our trust in rules and traditions,
and we long for you to release in the Church
such a desire to serve the living God
that nothing is allowed to get in the way of that.

Silence

Into your hands, O Lord:
we commit the future.

Father, we recognise in ourselves
the universal dangerous wants and cravings
which are cultivated because they make money.
Give us universally such a loathing of evil
that there is international co-operation
and individual responsibility in fighting it
and building one another up in love.

Silence

Into your hands, O Lord:
we commit the future.

Father, may our homes, schools and churches
reflect and engender the Godly values
of mutual care, respect and responsibility,
of integrity and forgiveness.

Silence

Into your hands, O Lord:
we commit the future.

Father, we stand alongside all who are hurting
in body, mind or spirit;
all who need courage, support or practical help.
Make us willing to become
part of your answer to our prayers for them.

Silence

Into your hands, O Lord:
we commit the future.

Father, as Lord of both time and eternity,
we commit to your keeping
those who have died to this life;
that, freed from all pain, and forgiven,
they may live in the peace and joy of heaven.

Silence

Into your hands, O Lord:
we commit the future.

Father, write your Law of love on our hearts
and send us glowing with thankfulness
through the week ahead.

Merciful Father,
**accept these prayers
for the sake of your Son,
our Saviour Jesus Christ. Amen.**

PROPER 18

Sunday between 4 and 10 September inclusive

Jesus comes fulfilling the hope of healing to wholeness;
he shows that mercy has triumphed over judgement.

Let us pray to our loving and merciful God.

Lord, we thank you for the richness and diversity
of each unique identity.
We pray for the separate members
of this Body of Christ, and our corporate nature,
that we may be filled at every level
with the living breath of God.

Silence

Father of mercy:
let your kingdom come.

We thank you for the beauty and variety
of our landscapes and cultures, all over the world;
for starscapes and the wideness of space.
Teach us to cherish and respect
this universe we inhabit
and all those who look or sound different
from ourselves.

Silence

Father of mercy:
let your kingdom come.

We thank you for the hope
each newborn child brings;
for the gentle gifts of laughter and friendship,
thoughtfulness and sympathy.
We pray that our eyes may see all others
with God's affection.

Silence

Father of mercy:
let your kingdom come.

We thank you for the patient endurance
of so many who suffer so much;
for them all we pray your wholeness
and refreshing,
your upholding and healing.

Silence

Father of mercy:
let your kingdom come.

We thank you for the promise of mercy
triumphing over judgement,
and commend to your love for ever
our own loved ones who have died.

Silence

Father of mercy:
let your kingdom come.

We thank you for all our blessings
and pray that we may take none of them
for granted,
but commit ourselves to live out
our thanks each day.

Merciful Father,
accept these prayers
for the sake of your Son,
our Saviour Jesus Christ. Amen.

PROPER 19

Sunday between 11 and 17 September inclusive

*Loving obedience to God is shown by Jesus
to be a quality rich in courage and wisdom,
a quality to be highly respected.*

As sons and daughters of our heavenly Father,
responding to his call,
let us bring to him our needs and concerns.

That we may all learn to think God's way
and desire to do his will above everything else;
that we may be ready to suffer if necessary,
and put ourselves out, and do that cheerfully,
considering it a privilege.

Silence

In the spirit of obedience:
we ask your guidance.

That the craving to be most powerful
may be transformed into a yearning
for mutual respect and harmony;
that wealth may not shout louder than right,
and the whisper of truth may be heard
above the clamour of expediency.

Silence

In the spirit of obedience:
we ask your guidance.

That within our homes and places of work
we may practise self-discipline in all that we say,
and in the way it is said,
using our mouths to speak wisely and positively
with love in both hearts and voices.

Silence

In the spirit of obedience:
we ask your guidance.

That those whose bodies or spirits
are heavy with suffering
may be given courage and hope,
ease from the pain, and healing to wholeness.
That we may know how best to help them.

Silence

In the spirit of obedience:
we ask your guidance.

That those who have died in faith
may rise to eternal life,
and that we may so live on earth
that we are all prepared
for meeting you face to face in heaven.

Silence

In the spirit of obedience:
we ask your guidance.

That, as we rejoice in the perfect love
and obedience of Jesus,
we may find his life transforming ours.

Merciful Father,
accept these prayers
for the sake of your Son,
our Saviour Jesus Christ. Amen.

PROPER 20

Sunday between 18 and 24 September inclusive

*The truly great in God's eyes are those who are
prepared to be last of all and servant of all.*

Let us pray to the God of glory
in whom we live and move and have our being.

We pray that the Church may hold true
to the teaching of Jesus, without being persuaded
that worldly values of status and ambition
are suitable or acceptable in Christ's followers.
We pray for a spirit of humility
to deflate all pomposity and arrogance.

Silence

Yours, Lord, is the kingdom:
yours the power and yours the glory.

We pray that all in positions of power,
authority and influence in our world
may recognise their calling to servanthood
and never lose their identity
with the needs and longings of those they serve.

Silence

Yours, Lord, is the kingdom:
yours the power and yours the glory.

We pray that all communities
may look after one another,
supporting the vulnerable, encouraging the timid,
providing practical help for all who need it,
and nurturing the young in a climate of trust.

Silence

Yours, Lord, is the kingdom:
yours the power and yours the glory.

We pray that none may be considered expendable,
or beyond our cherishing;
we pray for all who have lost heart,
through pain, suffering or sin,
that God's redeeming power may work its wonders
in the very darkest situations.

Silence

Yours, Lord, is the kingdom:
yours the power and yours the glory.

We pray that all who have wearily
struggled to death
may know the joy of burdens laid down,
and new, lasting life transforming them
through the eternal love of God.

Silence

Yours, Lord, is the kingdom:
yours the power and yours the glory.

We pray that we may find new joy
in giving and serving freely, without thanks,
rejoicing in the privilege of following Jesus.

Merciful Father,
accept these prayers
for the sake of your Son,
our Saviour Jesus Christ. Amen.

PROPER 21

Sunday between 25 September and 1 October inclusive

*Don't let your body lead you into sin and risk
exchanging eternal life for eternal punishment.*

Conscious of our need for God's power
in our lives, our Church and our world,
let us pray to him now.

Father, as you have called us to be salt,
give us the courage to reject sin and evil
in our own lives
and in the corporate life of the Church.
May our churches be powerhouses of your Spirit,
training and upholding us
as we live your life in the world.

Silence

Your Law, O Lord, is perfect:
it revives the soul.

Father, we pray for a greater awareness
of what damages souls and encourages evil,
and for widespread commitment
to addressing the dangers.
We pray for all who earn their living
through selling what destroys lives.

Silence

Your Law, O Lord, is perfect:
it revives the soul.

Father, we pray for the young,
and the vulnerable in every community,
for all in positions of trust,
for child-minders, playgroups and schools,
for children's clubs and the uniformed organisations,
for loving nurture and protection from all evil.

Silence

Your Law, O Lord, is perfect:
it revives the soul.

Father, we pray for all long-term carers
and those they look after,
for all who are having to learn dependence gracefully,
and those who are imprisoned by their guilt.
Work your healing love in them all,
reassuring them of your presence.

Silence

Your Law, O Lord, is perfect:
it revives the soul.

Father, we pray that no one may be lost eternally,
that all may turn from their sin and trust your mercy;
that physical death may be but the gate to heaven.
We commend to your love
those who have recently died.

Silence

Your Law, O Lord, is perfect:
it revives the soul.

Father, we offer you our thanks and praise
for sins forgiven, and the joy
of walking through life in your company.

Merciful Father,
accept these prayers
for the sake of your Son,
our Saviour Jesus Christ. Amen.

PROPER 22

Sunday between 2 and 8 October inclusive

*Human beings are made responsible for the care of creation
but are subject to God in all aspects of their lives.*

Let us come before God our Maker,
making our prayers to him,
through Jesus and in the power of the Holy Spirit.

We pray that the Church may be alive
to God's beckoning,
quick to obey his will
and always ready to act in his loving service
for the good of the world.

Silence

Lord of heaven:
let your will be done.

We pray that all leaders and heads of state
may take wise advice and act responsibly
for the well-being of all.
We pray for God's guidance
in the way we manage and care for this planet,
its resources, riches and inhabitants.

Silence

Lord of heaven:
let your will be done.

We pray for all marriages,
for those seeking marriage partners
and those whose marriages are under strain.
We pray for all in close relationships,
that there may be mutual love and respect.

Silence

Lord of heaven:
let your will be done.

We pray for all who are suffering
through illness, accident or deliberate cruelty;
for refugees and all who are abused;
that through the caring of human hands
they may experience the caring hands of God.

Silence

Lord of heaven:
let your will be done.

We pray for all who have died violently
or suddenly, or with no one to miss them.
May all who have died in faith
be judged with mercy
and welcomed into eternal life.

Silence

Lord of heaven:
let your will be done.

We pour out our thanks and praise
for the gift of life
and the gift of one another.
May we treat each other with renewed reverence.

Merciful Father,
accept these prayers
for the sake of your Son,
our Saviour Jesus Christ. Amen.

PROPER 23

Sunday between 9 and 15 October inclusive

*The word of God is living and active, piercing right to
the heart; only with God is it possible to be saved.*

Let us lay down our own agendas
and seek the face of God,
and his will for the Church and for the world.

We pray for all who are seeking God,
and for the nurturing process in this parish.
We pray for opportunities to share God's love
and draw others to meet him.

Silence

Your will be done:
on earth as in heaven.

We pray for all who are fighting against evil
for goodness, truth and justice,
both those who make the world news
and those whose battles are known only to God.
We pray for our country and its leaders,
that this nation may seek God.

Silence

Your will be done:
on earth as in heaven.

We pray that wealth and comfort may not divert us
from searching out the heart of God;
that we may hear God's challenging
and gladly respond to him;
that our homes and communities
may sparkle with God's glory.

Silence

Your will be done:
on earth as in heaven.

We pray for the disillusioned and depressed
and all who have lost their way in life;
we pray for those corrupted by evil,
trained in hatred and twisted by bitterness.
We pray for the transforming of these lives.

Silence

Your will be done:
on earth as in heaven.

We pray for those whose earthly life
has come to an end,
and for those who mourn their going.
May the dead rest in the peace and joy of heaven
through the mercy of God.

Silence

Your will be done:
on earth as in heaven.

With thankful hearts we recall the times
when God has rescued and forgiven us,
leading us deeper into his friendship.

Merciful Father,
accept these prayers
for the sake of your Son,
our Saviour Jesus Christ. Amen.

PROPER 24

Sunday between 16 and 22 October inclusive

*Even the Son of Man himself came not to be served
but to serve, and to give his life as a ransom for many.*

In humility and love, let us pray together
to the God of our making and redeeming.

That all Christians may fulfil their vocation
to be servants, caring for the needs of others,
obedient to their Lord in all things
and supportive of one another
in worship, prayer and deepening faith.

Silence

Into your hands, O Lord:
we commit our prayers.

That those who govern and advise
may seek out God's will
and the good of all
in each crisis, dilemma and debate.

Silence

Into your hands, O Lord:
we commit our prayers.

That we may develop the habit
of rejoicing in the opportunities to serve,
and to put ourselves out for others,
laying down our craving for praise
and importance.

Silence

Into your hands, O Lord:
we commit our prayers.

That those who suffer in mind, body and spirit
may sense the Christ close beside them,
knowing his healing and resting in his love.

Silence

Into your hands, O Lord:
we commit our prayers.

That those who have died in faith
may be welcomed into the light of heaven,
and that all who are walking in sin today
may turn away from evil, and live.

Silence

Into your hands, O Lord:
we commit our prayers.

We thank you, Lord God,
for your long-suffering patience with us,
and the affectionate forgiveness
which lifts us to our feet whenever we stumble.

Merciful Father,
**accept these prayers
for the sake of your Son,
our Saviour Jesus Christ. Amen.**

PROPER 25

Sunday between 23 and 29 October inclusive

In Jesus, God gathers his scattered people
and opens their eyes to see.

As children of our heavenly Father,
trusting in his will and capacity to care for us all,
let us pray.

We pray for all pastoral care in the Church,
for the ministries of listening and counselling;
the sharing of grief; the freeing from guilt.
We pray for the grace to accompany
others to Christ's healing love.

Silence

What do you want God to do for you?
Lord, we want to see.

We pray for the healing of the nations;
for a recognition of our need of God
and a turning away from all that is evil.
We pray for all in authority and worldly power,
that they may be guided along right paths.

Silence

What do you want God to do for you?
Lord, we want to see.

We pray for an increase in love for one another,
that we may be better at recognising needs
and responding to them;
that we may give more time to those we love.

Silence

What do you want God to do for you?
Lord, we want to see.

We pray for those who are blind
or partially sighted,
and those who are spiritually or emotionally blind.
We pray for the opening of eyes to see God's way
and faith to trust him through good and ill.

Silence

What do you want God to do for you?
Lord, we want to see.

We pray for those whose eyes
have shut to this world,
that they may open to the brightness
and joy of heaven.

Silence

What do you want God to do for you?
Lord, we want to see.

We thank you, heavenly Father,
for drawing us to you
and stretching out your arms to us in welcome.

Merciful Father,
**accept these prayers
for the sake of your Son,
our Saviour Jesus Christ. Amen.**

ALL SAINTS' DAY

Sunday between 30 October and 5 November inclusive

Great is the rejoicing in heaven among the saints
of God as they worship their Lord in glory.

Let us still our bodies
and open our hearts and minds to pray.

We pray for all the saints on earth,
all those walking as friends of Jesus
through the light and shadows of life,
in grassy meadows and scaling bare rock;
that we may all persevere with joy,
supporting one another along the way.

Silence

Not our will, Lord:
but yours be done.

We pray for all the kingdoms and nations of the earth,
for their leaders and their people,
their policies and needs,
that under God's overarching love
they may learn his ways and his will.

Silence

Not our will, Lord:
but yours be done.

We pray for those we love and care for
and those who love and pray for us,
for the wisdom to learn
from all we experience in this life,
so that we are not damaged,
but rather grow from the difficult times.

Silence

Not our will, Lord:
but yours be done.

We pray for those who are suffering
and those too weak to pray;
for all who are searching for life's meaning
and those who find it hard to believe
they are loved and cherished by the living God.

Silence

Not our will, Lord:
but yours be done.

We pray for those who have died in faith,
giving thanks for the shining lives of the saints,
and asking that with them
we may come to share
in the endless joy of heaven.

Silence

Not our will, Lord:
but yours be done.

With thankfulness we celebrate
the transforming love of God,
which can take us as we are
and make us into what God can already see
we could become.

Merciful Father,
accept these prayers
for the sake of your Son,
our Saviour Jesus Christ. Amen.

FOURTH SUNDAY BEFORE ADVENT

Sunday between 30 October and 5 November inclusive*

* For use if the Feast of All Saints was celebrated on 1 November and alternative propers are needed.

To love the living God with heart, soul and strength,
and to love our neighbour as ourselves means far
more than any sacrificial offerings.

As God's people, gathered in his presence,
let us pray.

For all who preach and teach the Gospel
in word and sacrament
throughout the worldwide Church.
For those who lead prayer groups
and Bible studies,
and all who gossip their faith to others.

Silence

O Lord our God:
in you we trust.

For all who are tortured or persecuted
for what they believe;
for the voiceless and powerless,
for the powerful and coercive.

Silence

O Lord our God:
in you we trust.

For greater respect for one another
as children of God's making;
for God's presence in each conversation,
discussion and debate,
each concern and celebration.

Silence

O Lord our God:
in you we trust.

For healing and wholeness,
mending and comforting,
calming and refreshing,
wherever lives and bodies ache.

Silence

O Lord our God:
in you we trust.

For everlasting peace in the arms of God
for those who have come to the end
of their life on earth
and comfort for all who grieve.

Silence

O Lord our God:
in you we trust.

We give thanks for God's constant love
which upholds our being
and cradles our living in his hand.

Merciful Father,
accept these prayers
for the sake of your Son,
our Saviour Jesus Christ. Amen.

THIRD SUNDAY BEFORE ADVENT

Sunday between 6 and 12 November inclusive

*When we are called we need to respond with obedience
so that many may be brought to repentance.*

Let us pray to the God who has called us to be here,
bringing to him the cares of our Church and our world.

We pray for deeper faith among Christians,
and a readiness to respond to God's calling.
For those being called to particular ministries
and those called to change their way of living,
we pray for courage, and the grace to obey.

Silence

Unfailing love is yours, Lord:
you are our rock of refuge.

We pray for all who feel pressurised
to conform to wrong values
in order to be accepted;
for a commitment to fight evil
and cultivate good in our world.

Silence

Unfailing love is yours, Lord:
you are our rock of refuge.

We pray for the households of this parish
and God's indwelling there;
for guidance in the everyday decisions
and the times of crisis.

Silence

Unfailing love is yours, Lord:
you are our rock of refuge.

We pray for the weak, the vulnerable,
the weary and the desolated;
for those entrenched in sin
and endangering others.

Silence

Unfailing love is yours, Lord:
you are our rock of refuge.

We pray for those who have died
in God's friendship,
and give thanks for their lives.
May they be called into the light of heaven.

Silence

Unfailing love is yours, Lord:
you are our rock of refuge.

In thankfulness we pray
for those who called us to repentance
and offered us the hope of new life in Christ.

Merciful Father,
**accept these prayers
for the sake of your Son,
our Saviour Jesus Christ. Amen.**

SECOND SUNDAY BEFORE ADVENT

Sunday between 13 and 19 November inclusive

We are to be on our guard; great anguish will accompany the last days, but all that is good and loving, wise and true will be saved and celebrated for ever.

As God's love has drawn us,
let us pray.

That the Church may grow and flourish,
protected from evil within and without;
that in worship and ministry
God's love may be brought into places of darkness
and offer many the light of hope.

Silence

Lord our God:
show us the path of life.

That our shrinking world
may bring about co-operation
and a fresh appreciation of one another's cultures;
that we may encourage one another
in goodness, peace and love.

Silence

Lord our God:
show us the path of life.

That we may take time
to cherish our loved ones in the present moment,
and value the blessings we receive each day.

Silence

Lord our God:
show us the path of life.

That God's healing touch
may bring wholeness and peace
to those who suffer,
and hope to those who are close to despair.

Silence

Lord our God:
show us the path of life.

That God's love may surround those
travelling through death
and bring them safely to heaven.

Silence

Lord our God:
show us the path of life.

We praise and bless you, Lord,
for Christ's saving death
and the promise of everlasting life.

Merciful Father,
accept these prayers
for the sake of your Son,
our Saviour Jesus Christ. Amen.

CHRIST THE KING

Sunday between 20 and 26 November inclusive

*Jesus Christ is the everlasting King whose
kingdom is not of this world, but grows in
the hearts of his people and lasts for ever.*

As children of the kingdom,
let us make our prayers to the eternal God,
who loves us.

We pray for your kingdom to come
in the worldwide communities
of those who believe in Jesus Christ –
may our lives enthrone him.

Silence

Spirit of the living God:
may your kingdom come.

We pray for your kingdom to come
in the nations of our world
and in their leadership;
for God's values to take root and grow;
for each person to be respected
as a beloved child of God.

Silence

Spirit of the living God:
may your kingdom come.

We pray for your kingdom to come
in our homes and families,
our neighbourhoods and places of work,
in all thinking, all speaking and all action.

Silence

Spirit of the living God:
may your kingdom come.

We pray for your kingdom to come
in all hospitals and surgeries,
and in every place of pain and sadness.

Silence

Spirit of the living God:
may your kingdom come.

We pray for your kingdom to come
in the final stages of earthly life,
in the journey through death,
and in the awakening to eternal life.

Silence

Spirit of the living God:
may your kingdom come.

We thank you for making us,
and redeeming us,
opening wide to us the gates of heaven.

Merciful Father,
accept these prayers
for the sake of your Son,
our Saviour Jesus Christ. Amen.

Year C

FIRST SUNDAY
OF ADVENT

*The gathered hopes of generations remind us to
get ourselves ready, so that Christ's return
will be a day of excitement and great joy.*

As we think about the fulfilment of all things today,
let us speak with the God of our making.

We pray that we will all be ready
to meet God face to face,
whenever that will be.

Silence

Lord, show us how to live:
and give us the courage to go forward.

We pray that all who lead and advise
may be led and advised by you,
so that our decisions are in line with your compassion.

Silence

Lord, show us how to live:
and give us the courage to go forward.

We pray that our families and neighbours
may be brought into contact
with the one true, living God
and know his affection for them.

Silence

Lord, show us how to live:
and give us the courage to go forward.

We pray that those hurt by injustice
may know your support,
and that the frail and timid
may know your encouragement and reassurance.

Silence

Lord, show us how to live:
and give us the courage to go forward.

We pray that those moving into eternity
through the gate of death
may be welcomed,
and their grieving loved ones comforted.

Silence

Lord, show us how to live:
and give us the courage to go forward.

We look with hope
to the fulfilment of all you have done,
and offer you our thanks and praise
for all your love.

Merciful Father,
accept these prayers
for the sake of your Son,
our Saviour Jesus Christ. Amen.

SECOND SUNDAY OF ADVENT

*It had been prophesied that there would be a
messenger to prepare the way for the coming of
the Messiah. Now John the Baptist appears
with his urgent message of repentance.*

We know that God is here with us,
and hears what is in our thoughts and in our hearts.

So we pray for all who claim to be Christians
all over the world.
We ask for a real longing for God in our lives;
a longing that is not satisfied by anything else.

Silence

Holy God:
we want to know you better.

We pray for the different countries
and those with power and influence.
We pray for honesty, justice and integrity.

Silence

Holy God:
we want to know you better.

We pray for those we love
and those we find it hard to relate to.
We pray for more love and forgiveness.

Silence

Holy God:
we want to know you better.

We pray for those in pain
and those imprisoned by addiction.
We pray for healing, wholeness and freedom.

Silence

Holy God:
we want to know you better.

We pray for those who have died
and now see you face to face.
We pray for those who miss them here.

Silence

Holy God:
we want to know you better.

We thank you for showing us
what needs putting right,
and for forgiving us all that is past.

Merciful Father,
accept these prayers
for the sake of your Son,
our Saviour Jesus Christ. Amen.

THIRD SUNDAY OF ADVENT

*Our period of preparation shifts from repentance
and forgiveness to the freed exhilaration of hope,
as the momentous truth of God's immanence
begins to dawn on us.*

God is here with us now.
Let us pray.

Father, we want to be ready to receive you.
Take us as we are and cultivate in us
a heart that longs for you and worships you
above and beyond everything else.

Silence

Come, O come:
Emmanuel, God with us.

We open to your love
the spiritual journeys of all who walk your way;
protect them from evil
and keep them steadfast in faith.

Silence

Come, O come:
Emmanuel, God with us.

We pray for those who give us support
and encourage us and listen to us
and make us laugh and share our sorrows.
Bless their lives and give them joy.

Silence

Come, O come:
Emmanuel, God with us.

We remember in God's presence
those whose memories are painful,
and those whose bitter resentment
cramps and distorts present relationships.
We ask for the healing only God can give.

Silence

Come, O come:
Emmanuel, God with us.

We call to mind those we know who have died,
and any who are close to death at the moment.
As they meet the one true God
open their hearts to receive his love,
mercy and forgiveness.

Silence

Come, O come:
Emmanuel, God with us.

We give God thanks
for the way none of us is beyond his saving love
and the way he has promised
to keep us ultimately safe.

Merciful Father,
accept these prayers
for the sake of your Son,
our Saviour Jesus Christ. Amen.

FOURTH SUNDAY OF ADVENT

When we co-operate with God
amazing things happen.

As we share in Mary and Elizabeth's joy
at the coming of our Saviour,
let us quieten and still ourselves
in the presence of God.

Heavenly Father, we can only marvel
at the way you are happy to work with us.
We want you to know
that we are willing to be used.

Silence

Let it be to me:
according to your will.

We call to mind before you
those whom we would love to know you
and we ask you to prepare their hearts
to recognise you.

Silence

Let it be to me:
according to your will.

We ask you to reassure and encourage us in this parish,
giving us insights to the real needs
and what you would have us do.

Silence

Let it be to me:
according to your will.

We ask you to give us courage
to continue working with you
even during the dark and dangerous times.

Silence

Let it be to me:
according to your will.

We call to mind those who are struggling
with poverty, illness or despair,
and ask you to comfort them,
using us however you want.

Silence

Let it be to me:
according to your will.

We remember those who have died
and thank you for the good
you have worked in their lives.
May we, with them, share in the life with you
that lasts for ever.

Silence

Let it be to me:
according to your will.

As we approach the festival of Christmas,
we praise and thank you for the full provision
you have given us
through the coming of Jesus.

Merciful Father,
accept these prayers
for the sake of your Son,
our Saviour Jesus Christ. Amen.

CHRISTMAS DAY

*Emmanuel – 'God with us' – is born at Bethlehem into
the human family. Now we will be able to understand,
in human terms, what God is really like.*

Emmanuel, God with us:
we welcome you!

As we celebrate God's coming to us
as a human child,
we bring the needs of our world
before the God we can trust.

We pray for all those who worship God
in every country of our world.
We pray for the grace
to know and love God more deeply.

Silence

Emmanuel, God with us:
we welcome you!

We pray for those who are spending this Christmas
apart from those they love.
We pray for those whose celebrations
are tempered with sorrow or fear.

Silence

Emmanuel, God with us:
we welcome you!

We pray for peace in the Holy Land
and for all who now live in the city of Bethlehem.

Silence

Emmanuel, God with us:
we welcome you!

We pray for those working over Christmas,
for all women giving birth
and all babies being born today.
We pray for their homes and families.

Silence

Emmanuel, God with us:
we welcome you!

We pray for those being born into eternal life
through the gate of death,
and commend them to God's love and mercy.

Silence

Emmanuel, God with us:
we welcome you!

Thank you, heavenly Father,
for the extraordinary love you show for us
in entering our world
through the natural channel of birth.

Merciful Father,
accept these prayers
for the sake of your Son,
our Saviour Jesus Christ. Amen.

FIRST SUNDAY OF CHRISTMAS

*Jesus' perception and understanding of his purpose and
work begins to take shape throughout his childhood.*

Incarnate God:
we love you and we need you.

We have been called
to pray for one another in God's presence.
Let us settle ourselves to do that now.

We pray for all who are called to lead and teach
so that the truth of God's love
is shared throughout the world.
We ask for wisdom, energy
and sensitivity to God's prompting.

Silence

Incarnate God:
we love you and we need you.

We pray for all with power
and influence in our world.
We ask for a widespread desire
for those qualities of compassion and integrity.

Silence

Incarnate God:
we love you and we need you.

We pray for all parents and their children,
especially where there are conflicts,
anxious moments and gaps in communication.

Silence

Incarnate God:
we love you and we need you.

We pray for all missing persons and their families,
all who are rethinking their direction,
all who find life full of contradictions
at the moment.

Silence

Incarnate God:
we love you and we need you.

We pray for those who have come to the end
of their earthly life,
especially any who are unprepared.

Silence

Incarnate God:
we love you and we need you.

We give thanks and praise
for God's involvement in our lives.

Merciful Father,
**accept these prayers
for the sake of your Son,
our Saviour Jesus Christ. Amen.**

SECOND SUNDAY OF CHRISTMAS

Christ is the way God tells people about himself.

We have met here
in the real presence of our God.
Let us pray to him now.

Silence

Though we cannot see you:
your love surrounds us.

We bring to mind the worldwide Christian Church,
both leaders and people,
as we begin another year.
We ask for a deeper awareness
of your presence among us.

Silence

Though we cannot see you:
your love surrounds us.

We bring to mind the troubled areas of our world
where corruption, injustice and violence
ruin lives and damage self worth.
We ask for your renewing and cleansing.

Silence

Though we cannot see you:
your love surrounds us.

We call to mind those we have spent time with
over this Christmas season;
the good and the disturbing conversations,
the joys and the aches of those we love.

Silence

Though we cannot see you:
your love surrounds us.

We bring to mind all who live away from home,
all refugees and all children in care.
We ask for the security that only you can give.

Silence

Though we cannot see you:
your love surrounds us.

We bring to mind those who have died recently
and all who grieve for them.
We ask for comfort to be given to the dying
and the assurance of your presence.

Silence

Though we cannot see you:
your love surrounds us.

We bring to mind the risks you were prepared to take
in becoming one of us out of love for us,
and we offer you our thanks and praise.

Merciful Father,
accept these prayers
for the sake of your Son,
our Saviour Jesus Christ. Amen.

THE EPIPHANY

Jesus, the hope of the nations,
is shown to the world.

We are all companions on a spiritual journey.
As we travel together, let us pray.

Silence

Light of the world:
shine in our darkness.

We pray that the worldwide Church
may always be ready
to travel in your way
and in your direction.

Silence

Light of the world:
shine in our darkness.

We pray for the nations
as they live through conflicts
and struggle with identity.
We long for all peoples
to acknowledge the true and living God.

Silence

Light of the world:
shine in our darkness.

We pray for the families and the streets we represent,
asking for a spirit of generous love,
understanding and mutual respect.

Silence

Light of the world:
shine in our darkness.

We pray for all who are finding their way
tedious, lonely or frightening at the moment;
for those who have lost their way
and do not know what to do for the best.

Silence

Light of the world:
shine in our darkness.

We pray for those who have come
to the end of their earthly journey,
and for those who have died unprepared.

Silence

Light of the world:
shine in our darkness.

We offer our thanks and praise
for the way you see us when we are still far off
and welcome us home.

Merciful Father,
**accept these prayers
for the sake of your Son,
our Saviour Jesus Christ. Amen.**

THE BAPTISM OF CHRIST
FIRST SUNDAY OF EPIPHANY

*Jesus is baptised, and God confirms
his identity and his calling.*

Let us pray to the God
who calls us each by name.

We pray for all baptised Christians
to live out their calling in loving and holy lives.
We pray for those preparing
for Baptism and Confirmation;
for parents and godparents
to be given the grace and perseverance
to keep faithfully the promises made.

Silence

Come, Holy Spirit:
fill our lives.

We pray for peace and integrity
in all our dealings as individuals,
and in local, national and international conflicts;
for openness to hear God's wisdom
and courage to follow his lead.

Silence

Come, Holy Spirit:
fill our lives.

We pray for harmony and understanding
in our relationships with family and neighbours;
for the willingness both to give and to receive,
for the generosity of forgiving love.

Silence

Come, Holy Spirit:
fill our lives.

We pray for those whose weariness or pain
makes it difficult for them to pray;
may they sense the support and love
of the Church of God.

Silence

Come, Holy Spirit:
fill our lives.

We pray for those whose souls
have left behind their frail and broken bodies
and can now fly freely to live in God's company
for the whole of eternity.
Bless and comfort their loved ones,
and bring us all in your good time,
to share the joy of heaven.

Silence

Come, Holy Spirit:
fill our lives.

We give you thanks for calling us by name
and keeping us safe
through all the storms and difficulties of this life,
in the power of the Holy Spirit.

Merciful Father,
**accept these prayers
for the sake of your Son,
our Saviour Jesus Christ. Amen.**

SECOND SUNDAY OF EPIPHANY

As a marriage celebrates the beginning of a changed,
new life for the bride and groom, so our loving,
faithful God has chosen us and is ready to transform
our lives for the good of the world.

Drawn by God's love and constant faithfulness to us,
let us pray.

We pray for all those who would love to believe
but cannot yet trust in the living God.
We pray for those who have rejected God
because of the unloving behaviour of his followers.

Silence

Fill us, Lord:
fill us to the brim.

We pray for all who give orders
and have influence over other people.
We pray that all peoples may be led justly
and with sensitivity.

Silence

Fill us, Lord:
fill us to the brim.

We pray for all our relationships
which need your transforming love;
we pray for those we irritate and upset
and those who have hurt and upset us.

Silence

Fill us, Lord:
fill us to the brim.

We pray for those whose lives feel empty
and lacking real meaning.
We pray for those whose frailty, pain or illness
makes it difficult to pray.

Silence

Fill us, Lord:
fill us to the brim.

We pray for those who are dying
and those who have completed their life on earth,
that they may be brought to peace and everlasting joy.

Silence

Fill us, Lord:
fill us to the brim.

We thank you for all the joys of loving relationships,
all the friendships we share,
and the love we are enabled to give.

Merciful Father,
**accept these prayers
for the sake of your Son,
our Saviour Jesus Christ. Amen.**

THIRD SUNDAY OF EPIPHANY

The meaning of the scriptures
is revealed to the people.

Let us still our bodies and our minds
as we pray together.

Silence

Open our ears, Lord:
and teach us to listen to you.

Lord God, as we call to mind
that we are members of the worldwide Church,
we pray for those who are insulted
or persecuted for our shared faith.
We stand alongside them now.

Silence

Open our ears, Lord:
and teach us to listen to you.

We pray that all of us
who inhabit planet Earth in this age
may learn to hear you again
and respond to your voice of love.

Silence

Open our ears, Lord:
and teach us to listen to you.

We pray that wherever materialism
or stress or sorrow or sin
have deafened us to your will,
we may be prompted to put things right.

Silence

Open our ears, Lord:
and teach us to listen to you.

We pray that our homes may be places
where you are welcomed and recognised
through the good and the troubled times.

Silence

Open our ears, Lord:
and teach us to listen to you.

We bring to your love all our fellow members
who are ill, injured or sad.
Alert us to see how we can help,
and give them a real sense
of your comforting presence.

Silence

Open our ears, Lord:
and teach us to listen to you.

We remember those who have travelled through life
and now have gone through death into eternity.
We thank you for their lives
and commend them to your keeping.
Prepare us all, through our living, for eternal life.

Silence

Open our ears, Lord:
and teach us to listen to you.

Thank you, Lord God, for all you have shown us
through Jesus, and through word and sacrament,
week by week.

Merciful Father,
**accept these prayers
for the sake of your Son,
our Saviour Jesus Christ. Amen.**

FOURTH SUNDAY OF EPIPHANY

At eight days old, Jesus is presented in the temple,
and at the Purification is revealed to Simeon
and Anna as the promised Saviour who is
able to reveal to us our true selves.

As we gather in Christ's name,
let us bring to mind those
who particularly need our prayer support.

We remember those who teach the faith
throughout the Church and throughout the world.
Keep them close to your guiding,
and open the hearts of those they teach
to hear and receive your truth.

Silence

Show us your ways:
and help us to walk in them.

We remember those in positions
of authority and influence
in this country and in all societies,
that needs may be noticed and addressed,
good values upheld and all people respected.

Silence

Show us your ways:
and help us to walk in them.

We remember those who looked after us
when we were very young,
and those who have no one to love and care for them.
We remember all young families
and all the children in our parish,

that they may be introduced to the one true God
and live their lives in his company.

Silence

Show us your ways:
and help us to walk in them.

We remember the elderly faithful
and especially those who are housebound
and can no longer join us to worship in person.
We thank you for their example
and ask you to increase our love for one another
across the age groups.

Silence

Show us your ways:
and help us to walk in them.

We remember those who have finished their lives on earth
and commit them to your everlasting care and protection.
We ask you to keep us faithful to the end of our life.

Silence

Show us your ways:
and help us to walk in them.

We remember with thankfulness
our elderly friends and relatives
and celebrate the way their lives
enrich our community.

Merciful Father,
accept these prayers
for the sake of your Son,
our Saviour Jesus Christ. Amen.

PROPER 1

God calls his people and commissions them.

Let us pray together in the presence of our God.

We pray for all who have been called
to be workers in God's harvest,
searching for the lost and loving them into the kingdom.
We pray for those who teach God's love,
both by word and by the way they live.

Silence

Here I am, Lord:
ready for your service!

We pray for those in authority
and in positions of power,
that under their leadership
there may be mutual respect, integrity and justice.
We pray for discernment
to see where injustice needs righting
and when we need to speak out.

Silence

Here I am, Lord:
ready for your service!

We pray for families suffering poverty
or financial difficulties,
for families full of tension and disagreement,
and for families coping with grief or separation.
We pray for the extended families represented here.
We pray for better awareness
of how our behaviour affects others.

Silence

Here I am, Lord:
ready for your service!

We pray for those who have been working all night
and all who work long hours in poor conditions.
We pray for those who have no work and feel rejected.
We pray for any resisting what God is calling them into.

Silence

Here I am, Lord:
ready for your service!

We pray for those who have died
and those who grieve for the loss of their company.
We ask for the opportunity to prepare for death
by the way we live from now on.

Silence

Here I am, Lord:
ready for your service!

We thank you for the way you show us ourselves
and still accept us with love.

Merciful Father,
**accept these prayers
for the sake of your Son,
our Saviour Jesus Christ. Amen.**

PROPER 2

The challenges and rewards of living by faith.

Knowing our need of God,
let us pray.

Father, we bring to mind our Church,
both here in *(name of town)* and throughout the world.
It is for right values and right priorities
that we pray, in all we decide and do.

Silence

Lord our God:
in you we put our trust.

We bring to mind all who lead and govern,
and all meetings where important decisions are made.
We pray that justice and mercy are upheld
in line with your loving will.

Silence

Lord our God:
in you we put our trust.

We bring to mind our circle of family and friends
with whom we share the good and the difficult times.
We pray for the grace to discern more readily
the good in each person and the gifts they have to offer.

Silence

Lord our God:
in you we put our trust.

We bring to mind those caught up
in the frenetic pressures of life,
and those who are stressed to breaking point.
We pray for insight and courage to change things.

Silence

Lord our God:
in you we put our trust.

We bring to mind the dying,
especially those who are alone,
and we remember those we know who have died.
May they and we share
in the everlasting joy of your presence.

Silence

Lord our God:
in you we put our trust.

We thank you, Father,
for all the wise teaching
you have given us through Christ.
Give us grace to be doers of the word
and not hearers only.

Merciful Father,
accept these prayers
for the sake of your Son,
our Saviour Jesus Christ. Amen.

PROPER 3

*Jesus teaches us to love our enemies
and forgive those who sin against us.*

God remembers our frailty;
let us pray to him now.

When conflicts threaten to disrupt our fellowship
in the church community,
deal with our frustrations and anger,
and give us the grace to forgive.

Silence

May we love one another:
as you have loved us.

When the luggage we carry from the past
interferes with our capacity to cope with the present,
heal the damage from our memories
and transform our experiences for good.

Silence

May we love one another:
as you have loved us.

When the differences in cultures
block our understanding of one another
and obstruct the peace process,
broaden our vision to discern the common ground.

Silence

May we love one another:
as you have loved us.

When the layers of resentment
have turned into rock,
dissolve them with the rain of your loving mercy.

Silence

May we love one another:
as you have loved us.

As those we have known and loved
pass through the gate of death,
have mercy on them,
and receive them into the joy
of your eternal kingdom.

Silence

May we love one another:
as you have loved us.

As we acknowledge the beauty
of loving even our enemies,
we thank you for the extraordinary love
you show us in Jesus.

Merciful Father,
accept these prayers
for the sake of your Son,
our Saviour Jesus Christ. Amen.

SECOND SUNDAY BEFORE LENT

*'He commands even the winds and
the water and they obey him.'*

Humankind has been brought into life by God.
We owe our very existence to him.
Let us pray to him now.

We pray for each living person
inhabiting our world with us,
with all the needs, emotions and experiences we share.
We pray that we may recognise one another
as brothers and sisters
sharing the same heavenly Father.

Silence

Lord of creation:
let your will be done.

We pray for greater reverence for God's creation
in the way we use and manage resources and wildlife.

Silence

Lord of creation:
let your will be done.

We pray for all of us in the ship of the Church,
that whenever storms rock the boat
and appear to threaten us,
we may trust God to bring us safely through.

Silence

Lord of creation:
let your will be done.

We pray for our children
and for all giving birth and being born today.
We long for the world they enter to be welcoming
and full of God's practical love.

Silence

Lord of creation:
let your will be done.

We pray for those who have chronic illness
and have to live in constant pain.
We ask for God's comfort
and reassurance to support them.

Silence

Lord of creation:
let your will be done.

We pray for those who have died,
thanking God for the example of lives well lived,
and for the total healing now received.

Merciful Father,
accept these prayers
for the sake of your Son,
our Saviour Jesus Christ. Amen.

SUNDAY BEFORE LENT

*God's glory makes Moses' face radiant, and it transfigures
Jesus as he prays on the mountain. Our lives, too, can
become increasingly radiant as the Spirit transforms us.*

As God's people,
let us pray to him now.

Father, we long to shine with your light.
Set our hearts on fire with love for you
and for one another.

Silence

May our lives proclaim:
that the Lord our God is holy.

Father, cleanse your Church of all hypocrisy,
and focus our attention on you,
so that divisions and barriers crumble to dust.

Silence

May our lives proclaim:
that the Lord our God is holy.

Father, send lives of light among the darkness
of injustice, corruption and despair,
and strengthen those who are already
shining in dark places all over the world.

Silence

May our lives proclaim:
that the Lord our God is holy.

Father, come into our homes
and make them places of welcome
where your love is woven into all our relationships.

Silence

May our lives proclaim:
that the Lord our God is holy.

Father, give courage to those
who have to suffer physical pain
or mental and emotional anguish.
Enable them to draw on your resources
and transform all our pain and sorrow.

Silence

May our lives proclaim:
that the Lord our God is holy.

Father, welcome into your kingdom of everlasting light
all who have come to the point of death.
Comfort those who miss their physical presence,
and bring us all to spend eternity
in the radiance of your presence.

Silence

May our lives proclaim:
that the Lord our God is holy.

Father, we thank you for the lives
of those who have directed us to you,
and for the way you never give up on us.

Merciful Father,
accept these prayers
for the sake of your Son,
our Saviour Jesus Christ. Amen.

FIRST SUNDAY OF LENT

*Following his baptism, Jesus is severely tempted out in the desert,
and shows us how to overcome temptation.*

As children of our heavenly Father,
who knows us so well and loves us completely,
let us pray.

Father, knowing our weakness in the face of temptation,
we ask for your strength and protection
so that, though we stumble,
we shall not fall headlong.

Silence

Lead us not into temptation:
but deliver us from evil.

Father, we pray for all those who are fighting temptation
and finding it difficult to resist.
We ask you to help them see clearly,
and equip them with all they need
to choose what is right.

Silence

Lead us not into temptation:
but deliver us from evil.

Father, we pray for the Church
as it struggles to steer a straight course
true to your calling.
We pray for wisdom and courage,
honesty and the willingness to be vulnerable.

Silence

Lead us not into temptation:
but deliver us from evil.

Father, we pray for those we love,
whose company we enjoy.
We pray too for those who irritate us
and those whom we annoy.

Silence

Lead us not into temptation:
but deliver us from evil.

Father, we stand alongside all those who suffer,
all whose lives are in chaos or despair,
and all who live in the dark prison of guilt.
We pray for your reassurance and peace,
your understanding and compassion.

Silence

Lead us not into temptation:
but deliver us from evil.

We pray for the dying,
especially the unnoticed and despised.
We pray for those who have gone through death
and now see you face to face,
that they may receive your merciful forgiveness
and know the joy of living with you for ever.

Silence

Lead us not into temptation:
but deliver us from evil.

Father, we thank you for the knowledge
that nothing is beyond your forgiveness,
and no one beyond the limits of your love.

Merciful Father
accept these prayers
for the sake of your Son,
our Saviour Jesus Christ. Amen.

SECOND SUNDAY OF LENT

If only we will agree to put our faith in God,
he will fill our lives with meaning
and bring us safely to heaven.

Confident that God knows and loves each of us,
and understands our situation,
let us pray.

We pray for a deepening personal faith
in all Christians,
and renewed faith for all who are besieged by doubt.

Silence

You are our God:
in you we put our trust.

We pray that the Church
may be vigilant and courageous
in upholding the Christian faith,
and sensitive to the language and culture
of each person seeking for God in their lives.

Silence

You are our God:
in you we put our trust.

We long for a thirsting after God in our society;
for right living, justice and mercy
to be valued and worked for.

Silence

You are our God:
in you we put our trust.

We long for our homes and neighbourhoods
to reflect God's love

in our practical caring,
our hospitality and our parenting.

Silence

You are our God:
in you we put our trust.

We pray for those whose emotional pain
makes it difficult for them
to accept God's love and forgiveness;
and for all who feel that there is no hope.
We offer ourselves to be available
where you need us.

Silence

You are our God:
in you we put our trust.

We commend into your loving mercy the dying
and those who have made the journey through death.
With them we long to share the eternal joy
of your presence in heaven.

Silence

You are our God:
in you we put our trust.

We give you thanks and praise
for the endless love and patience you show us;
whenever we turn away,
please turn us back to you.

Merciful Father,
accept these prayers
for the sake of your Son,
our Saviour Jesus Christ. Amen.

THIRD SUNDAY OF LENT

We have God's invitation to come and drink freely
of his Spirit, but if we keep refusing his offer
it will eventually be withdrawn.

As we thirst for God in our lives,
let us pray to him now.

Father, we thirst for your meaning
and your guidance
in all our work and worship and praise.
Fill us so full with your Spirit
that those we meet are drawn to meet you.

Silence

Living Spirit of God:
quench our thirst.

Father, in all the corruption and double standards
which damage and unnerve our world,
we thirst for your Spirit of truth, purity and goodness.

Silence

Living Spirit of God:
quench our thirst.

Father, we thirst for your Spirit of love
which notices needs,
considers no job beneath itself,
and delights in each person's gifts.

Silence

Living Spirit of God:
quench our thirst.

Father, we thirst for your Spirit of compassion
which binds up wounds,
supports the nervous and frail,
and visits the imprisoned and afraid.

Silence

Living Spirit of God:
quench our thirst.

Father, we thirst for your Spirit of life
as we call to mind those who have come
to the point of earthly death.
May they, and we in our turn,
find eternal refreshment and peace with you.

Silence

Living Spirit of God:
quench our thirst.

Father, may we thank you with our lives
as well as our lips
for the constant outpouring of your Spirit to us
throughout our lives.

Merciful Father,
accept these prayers
for the sake of your Son,
our Saviour Jesus Christ. Amen.

FOURTH SUNDAY OF LENT
MOTHERING SUNDAY

While we are here in this life, given one another
to care for, we can learn the lessons of mutual
love and support and shared suffering.

Gathered together as children in God's family, let us pray.

Lord, into our church community
pour the insight and discernment we need.
May we learn to love you more
as we learn to live and work in harmony,
focused on you and not on our divisions.

Silence

God our parent:
supply our needs.

Into the unease and weariness of our world
pour the reality and wholesome truth we need,
that we may learn mutual trust
and support one another in love.

Silence

God our parent:
supply our needs.

Lord, into the laughter and tears of family life
pour the freshness of your living presence,
as we work at our relationships
and deepen our love for one another.

Silence

God our parent:
supply our needs.

Lord, into the loneliness and pain
of those who feel rejected and unvalued
pour your compassion and reassurance,
that each person may know
the full extent of your love for them.

Silence

God our parent:
supply our needs.

Lord, may the dying know your reality
and find comfort and hope in you,
and may those who have died in faith
live for ever in the beauty of your holiness.

Silence

God our parent:
supply our needs.

Lord, may the way we live with one another
proclaim the truth of your constant love for us.

Merciful Father,
accept these prayers
for the sake of your Son,
our Saviour Jesus Christ. Amen.

FIFTH SUNDAY OF LENT

When we are privileged to share in Christ's suffering,
we also share in his new life.

God is present with us now.
Let us bring him our prayers and concerns
for the Church and for the world.

Loving God, breathe your life into the Church,
so that we speak your love to the world
and are willing to suffer and prepared for sacrifice.

Silence

Lord, through your love:
transform our lives.

Loving God, breathe your peace into the world,
so that we work together co-operatively,
sensitive to one another's needs and differences.

Silence

Lord, through your love:
transform our lives.

Loving God, breathe your patience and forgiveness
into our homes and all our relationships,
so that we learn to cherish and respect one another
and act with generosity.

Silence

Lord, through your love:
transform our lives.

Loving God, breathe your encouragement
into every suffering and every sadness,
so that the dark and painful times
become places of strong spiritual growth.

Silence

Lord, through your love:
transform our lives.

Loving God, breathe your welcome
deep into the souls of the dying,
so that death is only the door
leading to the joy of eternal life with you.

Silence

Lord, through your love:
transform our lives.

Loving God, breathe your grace
into our knowing and our feeling,
so that we rejoice each step of the way,
whatever the terrain.

Merciful Father,
accept these prayers
for the sake of your Son,
our Saviour Jesus Christ. Amen.

PALM SUNDAY

*As Jesus rides into Jerusalem on a donkey, and the crowds
welcome him, we sense both the joy at the Messiah being
acclaimed, and the heaviness of his suffering which follows.
Jesus' mission is drawing to its fulfilment.*

As we recall Jesus entering Jerusalem,
let us gather our thoughts to pray.

Father, as the crowds welcomed Jesus
and sang your praises,
we pray that many more will welcome you
into their hearts and lives over the coming year.
We pray for opportunities to spread your good news
and courage to take them.

Silence

You are our God:
we welcome you!

Father, we recall the donkey Jesus rode on,
and we pray for that real humility in our hearts
which treats status and image casually,
and truth and loving service seriously.

Silence

You are our God:
we welcome you!

Father, the children sang and shouted your praise,
and we pray for the children in our homes,
our city and our land.
May we not fail them
in the support and teaching they need.

Silence

You are our God:
we welcome you!

Father, the crowds were responding
to the healing love they had seen in action in Jesus.
We bring to you in our love and imaginations now
all those we would have brought to Jesus
for healing and help.
Give them comfort and reassurance,
wholeness and hope.

Silence

You are our God:
we welcome you!

Father, Jesus knew he was riding to his death.
We pray for all on that last journey,
especially those burdened with fear and guilt.
We commend to your eternal love all who have died,
thanking you for the blessings we have received,
and even for the grief
which is part of the love we share.

Silence

You are our God:
we welcome you!

Father, we, too, spread our coats on the road
as we express our thankfulness
for all you have done for us
and the amazing extent of your love.

Merciful Father,
**accept these prayers
for the sake of your Son,
our Saviour Jesus Christ. Amen.**

EASTER DAY

It is true. Jesus is alive for all time. The Lord of life
cannot be held by death. God's victory over sin
and death means that new life for us is a reality.

With joy in our hearts,
come, let us pray together.

We remember with gratitude
the presence of the Church
in remote and highly populated areas
all over the world.
We pray for all other Christians rejoicing today
in the wonder of the Resurrection.

Silence

Life-giving God:
give us new life in you.

We pray that we may recognise you
as we walk through our days,
and we ask you to disturb any complacency
which is blurring our spiritual vision.

Silence

Life-giving God:
give us new life in you.

We pray for the courage to speak out
against injustice and oppression;
we pray that our leaders may establish and uphold
right values and sensitive legislation.

Silence

Life-giving God:
give us new life in you.

We pray that those of our families and friends
who have not yet met you
may be drawn into your company and introduced,
so that they can enjoy your faithfulness and love.

Silence

Life-giving God:
give us new life in you.

We remember those whose lives
are filled with pain, anxiety or sorrow,
and ask you to come alongside them
and speak their name.

Silence

Life-giving God:
give us new life in you.

With the words of Resurrection fresh in our minds,
we commend to your eternal love
those who have died,
that they may live with you for ever.

Silence

Life-giving God:
give us new life in you.

Father, may our lips and our lives
express our thanks and praise to you
for rescuing us and setting us free to live.

Merciful Father,
**accept these prayers
for the sake of your Son,
our Saviour Jesus Christ. Amen.**

SECOND SUNDAY OF EASTER

Having seen Jesus in person, the disciples are convinced
of the Resurrection. We too can meet him personally.

In the knowledge that God is here present with us,
let us pray.

Father, we thank you for the gifts of sight and insight,
and ask you to be there in all our looking.
Help us always to see with eyes of faith, love and honesty.

Silence

Open our eyes:
to see things your way, Lord.

We pray for our bishops, priests and deacons
in their demanding ministry of love,
that they may be given all the support,
grace and anointing they need.

Silence

Open our eyes:
to see things your way, Lord.

We pray for the gifts of discernment and integrity
among all those who govern, advise and lead.
Clear away all self-centred ambition
to free our leaders to serve.

Silence

Open our eyes:
to see things your way, Lord.

Whenever we have eye contact with family, friends,
neighbours or colleagues,
be there in that communication,
and remind us of our calling to love one another.

Silence

Open our eyes:
to see things your way, Lord.

We call to mind those whose eyes are wet with tears
or tense with pain.
Help them to sense your reassuring love
which can bring us through the darkest of valleys.

Silence

Open our eyes:
to see things your way, Lord.

Jesus is the firstfruit
of the new and eternal life we are promised in you.
We commend to your love
those who have recently walked through death
into that promise, and thank you for the privilege
of knowing them here on earth.

Silence

Open our eyes:
to see things your way, Lord.

Father we thank you for loving us
right through death into new life,
and we rejoice in your victory over evil.

Merciful Father,
**accept these prayers
for the sake of your Son,
our Saviour Jesus Christ. Amen.**

THIRD SUNDAY OF EASTER

Those who know Jesus and recognise that he is the anointed Saviour are commissioned to go out as his witnesses to proclaim the good news.

Let us gather with our prayers
before the God who knows each of us by name.

Father, we thank you that your Church
is made up of real people,
that it is a school for sinners,
and that you can work with us and through us
straight away.

Silence

Here I am, Lord:
send me!

Father, we pray for the newly baptised
and those who have recently returned to you;
help us, as your Church, to support them well
and delight in them as members together
of the body of Christ.

Silence

Here I am, Lord:
send me!

Father, we pray for your strength and protection
against all hypocrisy and double standards
in our society.
We pray for a spirit of genuine service
among all who lead and in all areas
where we have authority.

Silence

Here I am, Lord:
send me!

Father, we pray that you will make
our homes and our relationships
places where people know,
by the way we look at them and treat them,
that they are valued, cherished
and respected for who they are.

Silence

Here I am, Lord:
send me!

Father, as we call to mind all who have learned
to regard themselves with contempt,
draw near to them and whisper their true name
so that they discern the truth
of your love and respect for them.
And use our lives to affirm one another.

Silence

Here I am, Lord:
send me!

We pray for the dying
and those who have recently died,
commending them to the joy
and safe-keeping of your love.
We give thanks for all those who know and love us
and help us grow in faith.

Merciful Father,
**accept these prayers
for the sake of your Son,
our Saviour Jesus Christ. Amen.**

FOURTH SUNDAY OF EASTER

*Asked if he really is the Christ, Jesus directs his
questioners to look at his life in action and see for
themselves that he and the Father are one.*

As members together of the body of Christ,
let us pray to the true and living God.

We pray for the nurture
of each member of the Church;
for the newly baptised and for all
in ordained and lay ministry,
that our love for one another may show
as we work for the coming of the kingdom.

Silence

Direct our hearts, O Lord:
to love you more and more.

We pray for the gift of discernment,
so that we recognise God's presence,
and reverence his face
in the faces of those we meet.

Silence

Direct our hearts, O Lord:
to love you more and more.

We hold before you our monarchy
and all those who govern our country
and make its laws,
that we may act responsibly and with compassion,
attentive to real needs and good values.

Silence

Direct our hearts, O Lord:
to love you more and more.

We pray particularly for homes
filled with suspicion and envy,
and ask for the healing of old hurts,
together with hope and perseverance
as people set out on paths of reconciliation.

Silence

Direct our hearts, O Lord:
to love you more and more.

We pray for those whose capacity for trust and love
has been damaged by other people's sin.
We long for your healing
so that all who are imprisoned by their past
may walk freely into your future.

Silence

Direct our hearts, O Lord:
to love you more and more.

We pray for those who have recently passed through death,
that you will judge them with mercy,
so that, made whole in your love,
they may know the joy of your eternity.

Silence

Direct our hearts, O Lord:
to love you more and more.

We give you thanks and praise
for the salvation and restoration
that is now possible for us
through Christ's victory over death.

Merciful Father,
accept these prayers
for the sake of your Son,
our Saviour Jesus Christ. Amen.

FIFTH SUNDAY
OF EASTER

Christ, breaking through the barrier of sin and death,
allows us to break into an entirely new way of living
which continues into eternity.

It is God's love that has drawn us here together.
Let us pray to him now.

Father, wherever Christians are fussing and arguing,
living outside your will
or without the responsible love you teach,
bring about deep cleansing, healing and renewing,
so that we can really be your body in our world.

Silence

Lord, you show us:
what loving really means.

Father, wherever injustice stifles human growth,
and selfish ambition distorts leadership,
bring about right and good government
throughout the world,
born of your wisdom and humility.

Silence

Lord, you show us:
what loving really means.

Father, as we watch our children growing,
remind us of our calling to grow more loving
in the ways we deal with conflict,
approach difficulties,
and address the needs of those we meet.

Silence

Lord, you show us:
what loving really means.

Father, in the places of long-term pain
and sudden shock,
of weariness, disappointment and fear,
bring about the peace which only you can give
and the comfort which speaks of hope.

Silence

Lord, you show us:
what loving really means.

Father, may the physical death of those we now recall
be nothing less than the gateway
to a new and lasting life in your love and protection.

Silence

Lord, you show us:
what loving really means.

So, heavenly Father,
we offer you our hearts
with all the love you find inside
and thank you for putting it there.

Merciful Father,
**accept these prayers
for the sake of your Son,
our Saviour Jesus Christ. Amen.**

SIXTH SUNDAY OF EASTER

*The continuing presence of God, as Holy Spirit,
leads us, as Jesus promised, into a personally
guided outreach to all nations.*

Drawn by the Holy Spirit,
we have arrived at this moment,
when we can pray together for the Church
and for the world.

Lord God, as members of your Church
in this generation,
we ask your guidance and blessing
for all our deacons, priests and bishops,
and all in training for lay and ordained ministry.
As the people of God, we ask for the gifts we need
for the work you need us to do.

Silence

You are with us:
every step of the way.

Lord God, this fragile, vulnerable planet
is so beautiful, and in such need of your guidance;
we pray for a deeper valuing
of our universe and of one another;
for your kingdom to come on earth as in heaven.

Silence

You are with us:
every step of the way.

Lord God, may our homes be centres of love,
acceptance and welcome;
we pray that you will make your home among us
in each room and each relationship.

Silence

You are with us:
every step of the way.

Lord God, we pray for all who are weighed down
with doubts, fears and misgivings;
all who are haunted by the past
or scared by the future.
We ask for them awareness of your constant presence
and courage to place their hand in yours.

Silence

You are with us:
every step of the way.

Lord God, as we remember those
whose earthly life has come to an end,
we pray that they, and we in our turn,
may recognise you in heaven
and live in your light for ever.

Silence

You are with us:
every step of the way.

Lord God, we give you thanks
for all the blessings you shower on us
along the way of life,
and for the painstaking guidance you provide.

Merciful Father,
accept these prayers
for the sake of your Son,
our Saviour Jesus Christ. Amen.

ASCENSION DAY

Having bought back our freedom with the giving of his life,
Jesus enters into the full glory to which he is entitled.

As we celebrate together, let us pray together.

God of love, as we celebrate this festival
of Jesus' entry into heaven as Saviour and Lord,
we pray for unity in the Church
and reconciliation and renewed vision.

Silence

Both heaven and earth:
are full of God's glory.

As we recall the shout of praise in heaven
as the Lamb of God appears,
we pray for all who are hailed as heroes
and given great honour on earth;
for all who worship anyone or anything
other than the true God.

Silence

Both heaven and earth:
are full of God's glory.

We pray for all farewells and homecomings
among our families and in our community,
and for all who have lost touch with loved ones
and long for reunion.

Silence

Both heaven and earth:
are full of God's glory.

We pray for those who are full of tears,
and cannot imagine being happy again;

we pray for the hardened and callous,
whose inner hurts have never yet been healed.
We pray for wholeness and comfort and new life.

Silence

Both heaven and earth:
are full of God's glory.

We commend to your eternal love
those we remember who have died,
and we pray too for those
who miss their physical presence.

Silence

Both heaven and earth:
are full of God's glory.

We praise and bless you, God of our making,
for the way you draw us deeper
into the meaning of life.

Merciful Father,
accept these prayers
for the sake of your Son,
our Saviour Jesus Christ. Amen.

SEVENTH SUNDAY OF EASTER

Jesus lives for all time in glory;
we can live the fullness of Resurrection life straight away.

Let us pray to the God who gives us so much
and loves us so completely.

We pray for a fresh outpouring of your Spirit
in all areas of the Church,
till our lives are so changed for good
that people notice and are drawn
to seek you for themselves.

Silence

We are your people:
and you are our God.

We pray for godly leaders and advisers
all over the world,
and for the courage to speak out
against injustice and evil.

Silence

We are your people:
and you are our God.

We pray for those affected
by our behaviour and our conversation,
that we may in future
encourage one another by all we say and do.

Silence

We are your people:
and you are our God.

We pray for those as yet unborn,
that the good news will reach them too;
we pray for those who have rejected God
because of the behaviour of his followers;
we pray for all who have lost their way.

Silence

We are your people:
and you are our God.

We pray for the dying,
especially those who are unprepared or frightened.
Welcome into your kingdom
those who have died in faith;
may they live with you for ever.

Silence

We are your people:
and you are our God.

Thank you, Lord, for the new life
you have enabled us to live.

Merciful Father,
**accept these prayers
for the sake of your Son,
our Saviour Jesus Christ. Amen.**

PENTECOST

As Jesus promised, the Holy Spirit is poured out
on the apostles and the Church is born.

As the Spirit enables us,
let us gather ourselves to pray.

May all Church leaders,
ordained ministers and the laity
be filled to overflowing
with love for your people,
and kindled with fresh zeal
for spreading the good news of the Gospel.

Silence

Spirit of the living God:
fall afresh on us.

May all those negotiating for peace
in the delicate areas of national conflict,
industrial disputes and entrenched bitterness,
be blessed with the peace of God,
tranquil and patient beneath the pressures.

Silence

Spirit of the living God:
fall afresh on us.

In our homes and places of work,
our schools and hospitals,
may there always be time
for the warmth of loving concern
and the comfort of being valued.

Silence

Spirit of the living God:
fall afresh on us.

Give help to all rescue workers and keep them safe;
may all who are trapped in damaged bodies or minds,
in poverty or tyranny, in earthquakes, floods or storms,
be brought to freedom and safety
and be aware of your love for them.

Silence

Spirit of the living God:
fall afresh on us.

We pray for those who have died
and all who mourn their going;
calm the fears of the dying
and have mercy on us all.

Silence

Spirit of the living God:
fall afresh on us.

We thank you, heavenly Father,
for the gift of your Holy Spirit among us;
and we look forward to the future
infused with your life.

Merciful Father,
accept these prayers
for the sake of your Son,
our Saviour Jesus Christ. Amen.

TRINITY SUNDAY

The unique nature of God is celebrated today,
as we reflect on the truth that God is Creator,
Redeemer and Life-giver.

Let us pray to the Father,
in the power of the Holy Spirit,
through Jesus, the Son.

We pray for all theologians
and those who teach the faith
in colleges and Bible study groups
throughout the Church.
We pray for godly wisdom and human insight.

Silence

Holy God:
help us to know you more.

We pray for peace and co-operation,
harmony and mutual respect
in all our dealings with one another
locally, nationally and internationally.

Silence

Holy God:
help us to know you more.

We pray for those who depend on us,
and those on whom we depend,
for our physical and spiritual needs.
Enable us to honour one another
as children of your making.

Silence

Holy God:
help us to know you more.

We pray for those who feel fragmented;
and for those forced to live apart from loved ones
through war, political unrest,
natural disasters or poverty.
We commend their pain to your comforting.

Silence

Holy God:
help us to know you more.

We remember those who told us of you
through their words and lives;
we think of those who have died in faith
and ask that we may share with them
in the joy of your presence for ever.

Silence

Holy God:
help us to know you more.

We give you thanks for meeting us where we are,
and travelling with us in person.

Merciful Father,
**accept these prayers
for the sake of your Son,
our Saviour Jesus Christ. Amen.**

PROPER 4

The good news we have been given is not just for us,
but to pass on to the rest of the world.

We have gathered here today
in the company of the true God.
Let us pray to him now.

Lord, we ask for your blessing and anointing
on all involved with mission and outreach,
both here and abroad, among children and adults,
as they commit themselves
to spreading the good news.

Silence

You are the living God:
let your will be done in us.

We pray for all who have influence and authority,
through their political standing, fame or wealth;
speak into their hearts of righteousness and justice,
integrity and compassion.

Silence

You are the living God:
let your will be done in us.

We pray that we may take seriously
our responsibilities for nurturing our children
and those who do not yet know God's love.
Transform our living to reveal that love.

Silence

You are the living God:
let your will be done in us.

Lord, we call to mind those in need
of comfort and reassurance,

all in pain and mental anguish.
We pray for the lapsed and the doubting
and those who need your good news this week.

Silence

You are the living God:
let your will be done in us.

Have mercy on those who have recently died
and those on that last journey now.
Bring us all safely to heaven
to live with you for ever.

Silence

You are the living God:
let your will be done in us.

Lord, we thank you for the good news we have received;
may we be ready to share our joy with others.

Merciful Father,
accept these prayers
for the sake of your Son,
our Saviour Jesus Christ. Amen.

PROPER 5

*Our God is full of compassion; he hears our crying
and it is his nature to rescue us.*

Let us bring to the God who loves us
our prayers and concerns for the Church and the world.

God of compassion,
take our hearts of stone
and give us feeling hearts,
so that we as the Church
may be more responsive
to the needs and sorrows around us.

Silence

God of love:
show us the Way.

God of wisdom,
teach all in authority,
inspire those who lead,
protect each nation from evil,
and further each right decision.

Silence

God of love:
show us the Way.

God of tenderness,
dwell in our homes
through all the times of joy
and all the heartaches and sadness,
teaching us to show one another
the love you show to us.

Silence

God of love:
show us the Way.

God of wholeness,
speak into the despair and loneliness
of all who struggle with life and its troubles;
reassure, affirm and encourage them,
and alert us to ways we can help.

Silence

God of love:
show us the Way.

God of peace,
be with the dying,
and as you welcome those who have died in faith
into the full life of your kingdom,
we, too, remember them with thanks and love.

Merciful Father,
accept these prayers
for the sake of your Son,
our Saviour Jesus Christ. Amen.

PROPER 6

*God has the authority and the desire to forgive our sins
completely and set us free from guilt.*

Knowing your love for us, Holy God,
we have come before you to pray together.

We pray for all who have the care of souls,
and are entrusted with helping others to repentance
and giving them good counsel.
We pray for those called to speak God's values,
whatever the danger and regardless of popularity.

Silence

Work in us, Lord:
work in us for good.

We pray for those who refuse
to allow injustice or evil to go unchallenged;
for all who are under pressure
to behave wrongly
or keep quiet about something they know to be wrong.

Silence

Work in us, Lord:
work in us for good.

We pray for more loving forgiveness
in all our relationships,
for more self-knowledge,
the grace to recognise where we are in the wrong,
and the courage to seek God's forgiveness.

Silence

Work in us, Lord:
work in us for good.

We pray for all imprisoned by guilt, resentment,
bitterness and self-pity,
that they may come to know the relief of being forgiven.
We pray for all innocent victims,
that their scars may be completely healed.

Silence

Work in us, Lord:
work in us for good.

We pray for those who have died
unprepared to meet you,
and for all who have died in faith.
Have mercy on us all.

Silence

Work in us, Lord:
work in us for good.

Thank you, Lord God,
for the wideness of your mercy
and the completeness of your forgiveness,
which restores us to you in such joy.

Merciful Father,
accept these prayers
for the sake of your Son,
our Saviour Jesus Christ. Amen.

PROPER 7

God is close through all our troubles,
and can bring us safely through them.

Let us pray to the faithful God who knows us already,
and loves us so much.

We pray that any barriers within the Church,
built up by fear or prejudice, misunderstanding or hurt,
may be broken down in Christ and unity restored.

Silence

Whatever our journey, O Lord:
walk with us on the way.

We pray for our world to be governed wisely and well,
with proper consideration
for the vulnerable and weak,
with co-operation, honesty and respect for all.

Silence

Whatever our journey, O Lord:
walk with us on the way.

We pray for the healing
of hurts and tensions in our families;
and for our friends,
thanking you for the blessings they give;
as friends of Christ, may we be
generous in our friendships.

Silence

Whatever our journey, O Lord:
walk with us on the way.

We pray for those disturbed by mental illness,
and for all who are rejected and despised.

We pray for all in desolate situations at the moment,
and ask for your comfort and healing.

Silence

Whatever our journey, O Lord:
walk with us on the way.

We remember those whose earthly life has ended,
and for those grieving for loved ones.
Enfold them in your love
and let them become aware of you beside them.

Silence

Whatever our journey, O Lord:
walk with us on the way.

We give you thanks, O Lord,
for the loving way you provide for us,
even during the darkest times.

Merciful Father,
accept these prayers
for the sake of your Son,
our Saviour Jesus Christ. Amen.

PROPER 8

When we are called to follow Jesus, that means
total commitment, with no half-measures.

Holy God, you have called us
to meet and pray together,
and here we are.

We pray for those called
to lay and ordained ministry in your Church,
and for those at present testing their vocation.
We lay before you the work that needs doing here
and ask you to provide people to do it.

Silence

We ask in Jesus' name:
give us grace to discern your answer.

We pray for those called to serve you
in positions of authority and influence;
for all leaders to see true greatness as service
and true strength as humility.

Silence

We ask in Jesus' name:
give us grace to discern your answer.

We pray for those called to marriage,
and those called to the single life,
for parents and grandparents,
sons and daughters,
for acceptance of what we cannot change
and strength to live the Christian life
in our present situation.

Silence

We ask in Jesus' name:
give us grace to discern your answer.

We pray for those whose lives
are full of disappointment, disillusion and discontent;
for all who struggle with great perseverance
in difficult circumstances.
We pray for your strength, encouragement and direction.

Silence

We ask in Jesus' name:
give us grace to discern your answer.

We pray for those called, through death, into eternal life
and freedom from all their pain and suffering.
Receive them with mercy
and welcome them into your kingdom.

Silence

We ask in Jesus' name:
give us grace to discern your answer.

We thank you, Holy God, for your promise
that where two or three are gathered in your name
you will grant their requests.

Merciful Father,
**accept these prayers
for the sake of your Son,
our Saviour Jesus Christ. Amen.**

PROPER 9

In Christ we become a new creation.

Let us bring our cares and concerns
before the God who loves us.
We pray for more workers
to gather in the harvest of the kingdom;
for our churches to be places of welcome
and wholesome spiritual nurture;
for a healthy balance of tradition and exploration.

Silence

Use us, Lord:
in the building of your kingdom.

We pray for our nation and the nations of the world;
for an upholding of godly principles and just laws,
for reconciliation, peace and mutual co-operation.

Silence

Use us, Lord:
in the building of your kingdom.

We pray for those among our families and friends
who have no idea of the new life you offer;
we pray for them to discover you
so they may share the joy of living in your love.

Silence

Use us, Lord:
in the building of your kingdom.

We pray for those suffering from leprosy
and other skin disorders,
for those disfigured by disease or accidents,
for the lonely, the confused and the outcasts.

Silence

Use us, Lord:
in the building of your kingdom.

We pray for the dying, and their loved ones,
for those who have passed through death,
and the families and friends who miss them.
Surround them with your love.

Silence

Use us, Lord:
in the building of your kingdom.

We praise you, Lord, and give you thanks
for the fullness of this new life
you have given us in Christ;
keep us renewed and filled with your Spirit.

Merciful Father,
**accept these prayers
for the sake of your Son,
our Saviour Jesus Christ. Amen.**

PROPER 10

Straighten your lives out
and live by God's standards of love.

Let us pray to God,
knowing we can trust him.

We pray that as Christians we may take to heart
the need to walk the talk,
and live out what we profess.
We pray that nothing may get so important to us
that it pushes God's values aside.

Silence

Father:
let only your will be done.

We pray that those in authority and power
do not lose touch with the needs of those they serve,
so that the poor and oppressed and vulnerable
are always given value and respect.

Silence

Father:
let only your will be done.

We pray for those in our families
whom we love and have hurt or upset;
we pray too for those who have hurt or upset us,
and ask for God's reconciliation and healing.

Silence

Father:
let only your will be done.

We pray for those who have lost hope
of being rescued, noticed or valued;

for the complacent who cannot see their poverty,
for the prejudiced who mistake blindness for sight.

Silence

Father:
let only your will be done.

We pray for our loved ones
who have reached the moment of death,
and thank you for the example of their lives.
We commend them all to your safe keeping.

Silence

Father:
let only your will be done.

We give you thanks, Lord God, for the hope
and encouragement you give us
on our journey of faith.

Merciful Father,
**accept these prayers
for the sake of your Son,
our Saviour Jesus Christ. Amen.**

PROPER 11

Against impossible odds
God has reconciled us to himself, in Christ.

Our God is always ready to listen.
Let us pray to him now.

Father, continue to pour out your gifts on the Church,
so that many may be saved
and our faith may grow strong
and bear much fruit.

Silence

God of Love:
we put our trust in you.

Look with mercy on the conflicts of our world;
realign our values and goals
until they are in line with your will,
and our laws and expectations reflect your justice and love.

Silence

God of Love:
we put our trust in you.

Bless our homes and families
and all our neighbours and friends;
train us to listen to one another with full attention,
and recognise one another's gifts.

Silence

God of Love:
we put our trust in you.

Encourage the hesitant, curb the overpowering,
heal the sick, refresh the exhausted,
soften the hardened hearts,

open the eyes of the complacent,
and comfort all who are sad.

Silence

God of Love:
we put our trust in you.

Welcome into your eternity
all those who have died in faith;
may we in our turn share with them
the joy of living with you for ever.

Silence

God of Love:
we put our trust in you.

Thank you, Lord our God,
for the hope you have given us through Christ,
which enables us to enjoy living in eternity
even while we still journey here.

Merciful Father,
accept these prayers
for the sake of your Son,
our Saviour Jesus Christ. Amen.

PROPER 12

*Keep asking for God's Spirit and he will
keep pouring out his blessing on you.*

Heavenly Father, as you have taught us, through Jesus,
we come to you in prayer.

We pray for all who uphold and teach the faith,
for young Christians in schools and universities,
for Christians witnessing to their faith at work,
for all in danger of persecution.
We pray for your strength and courage.

Silence

In all things, Father:
let your will be done.

We pray for discernment and wisdom
as we strive for international co-operation
in managing the world's resources;
for perseverance as we work
towards peace and reconciliation.

Silence

In all things, Father:
let your will be done.

We pray for the good sense
in our family and community life
that knows the difference
between generosity and indulgence,
between lenience and neglect of responsibility.

Silence

In all things, Father:
let your will be done.

We pray for all victims of abuse and tyranny,
for all who suffer long-term effects
of torture, war or disease;
we pray for the grace to forgive,
and for healing of body, mind and spirit.

Silence

In all things, Father:
let your will be done.

We pray for those who have died,
and particularly for those
who have no one to mourn their going;
for those who have died unnoticed.
We pray that they may rest in your peace for ever.

Silence

In all things, Father:
let your will be done.

Father, we thank you for all the gifts
you pour out to us each day of our lives;
keep us asking, and keep us seeking you.

Merciful Father,
accept these prayers
for the sake of your Son,
our Saviour Jesus Christ. Amen.

PROPER 13

True richness is not material wealth;
true security is not a financial matter.

Let us pray to God our Father,
knowing that we are all precious to him.

Father, we thank you for all those
who give to support the work of the Church;
bless our giving, guide our spending,
and help us to value the true wealth
of your abundant love.

Silence

The Lord is our shepherd:
there is nothing we shall want.

We pray for the world's economy;
for fair management and distribution of resources;
for fair trade and just wages;
for greater awareness and concern about injustice;
for a commitment to our responsibilities
as planet-sharers and earth-dwellers.

Silence

The Lord is our shepherd:
there is nothing we shall want.

We pray for all parents with young children,
thanking you for them
and asking you to bless and guide their parenting;
we pray for families in debt;
for those whose homes have been repossessed,
and those whose financial security
makes them forgetful of your love.

Silence

The Lord is our shepherd:
there is nothing we shall want.

We pray for those who are burdened
with financial worries
and all who struggle to make ends meet,
all over the world;
we pray for the emotionally and spiritually bankrupt,
and those who do not yet know God's love for them.

Silence

The Lord is our shepherd:
there is nothing we shall want.

We pray for those who have died,
and those on that last journey at this moment;
for a merciful judgement
and the everlasting joy of heaven.

Silence

The Lord is our shepherd:
there is nothing we shall want.

Father, we give you thanks
for the extraordinary generosity of your love for us,
which lasts beyond death into the whole of eternity.

Merciful Father,
accept these prayers
for the sake of your Son,
our Saviour Jesus Christ. Amen.

PROPER 14

Have faith in God, and get yourself ready to meet him.

As God's beloved children,
let us come to him and open our hearts to him.

Father, you know both our gifts as a congregation
and the needs of those in this parish,
and we ask you to bless our ministry in this place.
Strengthen and encourage all Church leaders
and deepen our faith and sure hope.

Silence

Lord our God:
we believe and trust in you.

Father, heal our nation and all the nations
of what is in the past and still corrodes the present,
so that we may build on good foundations
and learn to govern ourselves with honesty,
respect for one another and sensitivity to needs.

Silence

Lord our God:
we believe and trust in you.

Father, be present in the daily living
of our homes and in all our relationships;
make us more trustworthy in our friendships,
and strengthen our resolve to live our faith in action.

Silence

Lord our God:
we believe and trust in you.

We call to mind all whose capacity to trust
has been damaged;

for those who are victims of injustice or corruption;
for the very young and the very old,
the frail, the vulnerable and the bereaved.

Silence

Lord our God:
we believe and trust in you.

We remember those
who have completed their earthly life in faith
and have now seen you face to face.
May they know the peace of eternity;
we too look forward to sharing that life of joy.

Silence

Lord our God:
we believe and trust in you.

Thank you, Lord our God,
for the glorious hope you have set before us.

Merciful Father,
accept these prayers
for the sake of your Son,
our Saviour Jesus Christ. Amen.

PROPER 15

*When we fix our eyes on Jesus
our lives will reflect his nature.*

God is close to us as we pray.
He is attentive to us now.

Lord, whenever you weep over our harshness,
make your tears melt our hearts of stone.
Whenever you grieve over our double standards,
shock us into honesty again.
Make us receptive to your teaching,
willing to take your risks
and eager to run with our eyes fixed on Jesus.

Silence

Lead us, Lord:
to walk in your ways.

Whenever the news overwhelms us,
nudge us to fervent prayer.
Wherever leaders meet to negotiate peace,
be present at the conference table.
Breathe your values into our thinking,
tear down the divisive barriers
and renew us to lead the world into loving.

Silence

Lead us, Lord:
to walk in your ways.

Whenever tempers are frayed
and patience is wearing thin,
give us space to collect ourselves and try again.
Whenever the demands of family and friends
remind us of our limitations,
minister graciously through our weakness
and teach us the humility of apologising.

Silence

Lead us, Lord:
to walk in your ways.

Whenever people are enveloped by pain
or desolate grief or total exhaustion,
bring refreshment and peace, tranquillity and hope.
Wherever the grip of the past
prevents free movement into the future,
bring release and healing.

Silence

Lead us, Lord:
to walk in your ways.

Whenever the dying are fearful and distressed,
give comfort and reassurance on that last journey.
Bless those who care for them
and those who mourn their going.
In mercy receive the dead
into the life of your heaven,
and prepare us, through our lives now, for eternity.

Silence

Lead us, Lord:
to walk in your ways.

Holy God, we love the beauty and goodness
of your nature,
and thank you for the gift of your Spirit
to guide us to walk in your ways.

Merciful Father,
**accept these prayers
for the sake of your Son,
our Saviour Jesus Christ. Amen.**

PROPER 16

*God sets his leaders apart to challenge prejudices and
assumptions, and alert people to the truth.*

Let us pray to the God who has loved us
throughout our whole life.

Lord our God, broaden our vision of your nature
and help us respond to your calling,
whether it suits us or not,
and whether it is convenient or not.

Silence

Lord God:
you are our hope.

May the whole Church reflect your light and beauty
in the love for God and neighbour,
displayed in corporate worship
and individual godly living.

Silence

Lord God:
you are our hope.

May no corruption, cruelty or injustice go unchallenged
in any part of our world,
however unpopular the challenging may be.
May our society protect the vulnerable
and encourage mutual care and support.

Silence

Lord God:
you are our hope.

May our care of the very young and the elderly
imitate the faithful and generous caring of our God;

may we overcome our envies, jealousies and grievances,
so that in God's love we can look at one another face to face,
and practise the liberating work of forgiveness.

Silence

Lord God:
you are our hope.

May all whose bodies cause them pain or immobility
be affirmed in value by loving encounter
with Jesus and his followers;
and may those who are spiritually crippled
be set free to love and serve God.

Silence

Lord God:
you are our hope.

May those who have died in faith
live for ever in the joy and peace of heaven
as children of Promise;
and may those who miss their company
be comforted and supported.

Silence

Lord God:
you are our hope.

May our gratitude to the One who sets us free
be shown each day in the way we live and speak.

Merciful Father
accept these prayers
for the sake of your Son,
our Saviour Jesus Christ. Amen.

PROPER 17

*When we live God's way, both individually and as
a community, we will be greatly blessed.*

Let us do the work of prayer that God has asked of us.

As the body constantly breathes,
may the Church, the body of Christ,
constantly pray,
breathing God's life into all its members and activities.

Silence

The Lord is our helper:
we shall not be afraid.

As a new week begins in our world,
may wrong priorities be challenged and adjusted,
may our societies reflect God's concern
for righteousness, true justice and responsive love,
and may all leaders grow in humility,
attentive to the needs of those they serve.

Silence

The Lord is our helper:
we shall not be afraid.

As we call to mind our loved ones,
all who depend on us,
and those on whom we depend,
all with whom we laugh, cry, work or play,
cleanse and refresh our relationships
and give us greater love, understanding and forgiveness.

Silence

The Lord is our helper:
we shall not be afraid.

We think of those who are in prison,
locked in cells or depression or dysfunctional bodies;
we think of those in hospital wards and accident centres,
those unable to reach medical help
and those on long waiting-lists for operations;
as we think of them all, we pray for them all.

Silence

The Lord is our helper:
we shall not be afraid.

We remember the dying and those who love them;
we remember those whose earthly life has come to an end,
and we commend them to God's undying love.

Silence

The Lord is our helper:
we shall not be afraid.

With love in our hearts
for God our Maker and Redeemer,
we choose to walk in his ways
through this day and all our days.

Merciful Father,
accept these prayers
for the sake of your Son,
our Saviour Jesus Christ. Amen.

PROPER 18

Following Jesus is expensive –
it costs everything, but it's worth it.

Let us pray to the God who has watched our growing
throughout our lives, and loves us.

Lord, there is nothing hidden from you.
All our thoughts and plans and secret fears
are open to you, even when we try to hide them.
Deal with the doubts and misgivings
and fears of your Church,
with the love and mercy which are part of your nature.

Silence

Gracious God:
in you we can trust.

Lord, you feel for the oppressed and the forgotten;
you understand the damage which can lead to violence,
the insecurity which can lead to defensiveness,
and the neglect which can lead to lack of control.
Heal the nations; restore what has been lost;
and turn our hearts to discern your will.

Silence

Gracious God:
in you we can trust.

Lord, you see the point at which
discussions turn to arguments
and preferences to selfishness.
You know the love inside our hearts for one another
that sings and dances and aches and worries.
Work on us now in the depth of our being
and bless our loved ones with a sense of joy.

Silence

Gracious God:
in you we can trust.

Lord, you suffer with those who suffer
and weep with those who weep;
we, too, stand alongside them now
in whatever pain, distress or sorrow
is engulfing them,
longing for them to be comforted.

Silence

Gracious God:
in you we can trust.

Lord, your death and resurrection
proclaim the message of hope
amongst the tears of our grieving
for those who have died.
Welcome them into the eternal light of your kingdom.

Silence

Gracious God:
in you we can trust.

Lord, your way may be costly
but to whom else could we go?
For you alone have the words of eternal life,
and we offer you ourselves.

Merciful Father,
**accept these prayers
for the sake of your Son,
our Saviour Jesus Christ. Amen.**

PROPER 19

*Jesus does not avoid the company
of sinners but befriends them.*

Let us pray to the God who longs for all to be rescued.

Heavenly Father, thank you for our bishops,
priests and deacons, and all who are called
to the different ministries in the Church.
Bless them as they work in your service
and uphold them with your power.

Silence

God our shepherd:
all our needs are known to you.

Thank you for all peace initiatives
and every genuine attempt at negotiation
in conflict resolution.
May those who govern be governed by your love;
may those who lead be led by your directing;
may the whole world come to know its need of you.

Silence

God our shepherd:
all our needs are known to you.

Thank you, Lord God, for our families and friends,
those we meet each day and those we seldom see;
draw all our loved ones closer to you,
and search out those whose faith
is fragile or fragmented.

Silence

God our shepherd:
all our needs are known to you.

Heavenly Father, as we recall the needs
of those who are sad or lonely,
lost, or afraid of what they have become,
we pray for the knowledge of your love
to wrap warmly around them,
and your living presence
to bring them to a place of safety and hope.

Silence

God our shepherd:
all our needs are known to you.

Have mercy, Lord God,
on those who have recently died;
may they enjoy the eternal life of heaven,
where there is no more pain, sorrow or weariness,
and every tear shall be wiped away.

Silence

God our shepherd:
all our needs are known to you.

Thank you, heavenly Father,
for your long-suffering patience with us.

Merciful Father,
accept these prayers
for the sake of your Son,
our Saviour Jesus Christ. Amen.

PROPER 20

If you cannot be trusted with worldly riches,
or even small amounts of money, then you will
not be trusted with spiritual riches either.

As God has taught us, let us pray
for the coming of the kingdom in every situation.

We long for the Church to be pure and holy,
alight with God's love and compassion,
and free from behaviour which is unworthy
of God's chosen people.

Silence

God our Father:
let your kingdom come.

We long for the nations to be wisely governed,
with just laws and a sense of vision
which reflects the best of human nature.
We long for peace and mutual respect
in each community throughout the world.

Silence

God our Father:
let your kingdom come.

We long for our homes to be filled with God's love,
so we are happy to put ourselves out for others,
to listen with full attention, and to value one another.
We long to clear away anything in our life-style
which competes with God for our commitment.

Silence

God our Father:
let your kingdom come.

We long for those who feel neglected
or rejected by society
to know God's love and acceptance of them.
We long for all those in pain and distress
to be comforted and relieved.

Silence

God our Father:
let your kingdom come.

We long for the dying to recognise
their need of God and his power to save;
for those who have died to be judged with mercy
and rest in God's peace.

Silence

God our Father:
let your kingdom come.

We give you thanks, Lord God,
for your teaching and your example
which opens our eyes to your truth.

Merciful Father,
accept these prayers
for the sake of your Son,
our Saviour Jesus Christ. Amen.

PROPER 21

*Wealth can make us complacent so that we fail
to notice the needs of those around us.*

All our needs are God's concerns.
Let us pray to him now.

Father, make us a listening Church,
welcoming to the hesitant,
encouraging to the young,
sensitive to the differences and attentive to the needs.

Silence

God, in mercy:
hear us as we pray.

Father, make us a caring world,
wise in government,
honest in promises,
far-sighted in the management of resources,
and open-hearted in charitable giving.

Silence

God, in mercy:
hear us as we pray.

Father, make us a responsible community,
supporting our neighbours and friends,
sharing one another's sorrows and joys,
and opening our homes to your indwelling.

Silence

God, in mercy:
hear us as we pray.

Father, as we remember those
who have asked for our prayers,

take their needs and provide for them,
take their wounds and heal them,
take their suffering and comfort them.

Silence

God, in mercy:
hear us as we pray.

Father, as we call to mind those who have died,
may they know the welcoming of your love
into eternal joy.

Silence

God, in mercy:
hear us as we pray.

Thank you, Holy God,
for knowing our needs
even before we become aware of them ourselves.

Merciful Father,
**accept these prayers
for the sake of your Son,
our Saviour Jesus Christ. Amen.**

PROPER 22

God hears our distress and our crying,
and feels it with us.

Knowing that God hears our prayers,
let us share our concerns with him
for the Church and for the world.

Father, we pray for all in lay and ordained ministry,
as they labour for the growth of your kingdom on earth;
keep them strong in the faith,
provide them with the energy and resources they need,
and inspire them daily with your love.

Silence

Lord, you are our hope:
you are our strength.

We pray for all meetings, conventions, and conferences,
for all policy making and planning;
may delicate negotiations be sensitively led,
and painful decisions bravely and wisely taken.

Silence

Lord, you are our hope:
you are our strength.

We pray for those we have upset or angered,
and those who have upset or angered us;
we pray for those who worry us,
and those we love but seldom manage to see.

Silence

Lord, you are our hope:
you are our strength.

We pray for those who are far from home
and those for whom it is too dangerous to return home;

we pray for the lonely, the unhappy,
those in pain and those convalescing.

Silence

Lord, you are our hope:
you are our strength.

We remember those who have come
to the end of their earthly life,
and those whose lives feel bleak
and empty without them.
We pray for mercy and peace and comfort.

Silence

Lord, you are our hope:
you are our strength.

Thank you, Lord, for being there beside us
through all the dark and rocky places in our lives.

Merciful Father,
accept these prayers
for the sake of your Son,
our Saviour Jesus Christ. Amen.

PROPER 23

*God can always use even seemingly
hopeless situations for good.*

God has proclaimed his love for us.
We can trust him with all our cares and concerns.

Lord, heal the Church of all its splits and divisions,
and bless its growth towards unity;
heal it of all unhealthy introspection
and bless its commitment to loving outreach.

Silence

Have pity on us, Lord:
you alone can save us.

May our society be mindful of those
who have particular difficulties;
may our laws testify to our sense of justice,
honour and integrity;
may the world's leaders be wisely advised
and honestly motivated.

Silence

Have pity on us, Lord:
you alone can save us.

Walk about our homes with your gifts of peace,
patience, forgiveness and joy;
help us through the disappointments and tragedies,
and celebrate with us in all our festivities,
for you are our most honoured guest.

Silence

Have pity on us, Lord:
you alone can save us.

We pray for all suffering from leprosy
and other infectious and life-threatening diseases;
Give courage to the long-term and chronically ill
and give respite to those who are at their wits' end.

Silence

Have pity on us, Lord:
you alone can save us.

We remember those who have died,
and we think of their loved ones, who miss them.
May this earthly death be a birth
into the eternal joy of heaven.

Silence

Have pity on us, Lord:
you alone can save us.

With great thankfulness we praise you
for your constant faithfulness to us,
your recognition of our deepest thoughts,
and your desire for our healing and wholeness.

Merciful Father,
accept these prayers
for the sake of your Son,
our Saviour Jesus Christ. Amen.

PROPER 24

Don't get side-tracked;
always pray and don't give up.

Our help comes from the Lord.
Let us pray to him now.

Loving Father, we pray for those
who teach prayer and Bible study
at schools and colleges, retreat houses, and conferences,
and in churches and homes all over the world.
We pray that many will find your words
speaking into their situation
and providing the guidance they need.

Silence

Lord, we love your ways:
our help comes from you.

We pray for those picking their way
through situations of potential conflict and danger;
for law makers and keepers
and all who are oppressed unjustly;
for the leaders of the nations and their people.

Silence

Lord, we love your ways:
our help comes from you.

We pray for the grace to listen to one another
and respond to one another's needs;
we pray for a spirit of co-operation and generosity
in our homes and neighbourhoods.

Silence

Lord, we love your ways:
our help comes from you.

We pray for those who are wrestling with problems
which seem too big to cope with;
for those who have recently received news
that has stunned or appalled them,
and are still in a state of shock.

Silence

Lord, we love your ways:
our help comes from you.

We pray for those who have gone through death,
that they may be judged with mercy
and brought safely into the eternal life of heaven.

Silence

Lord, we love your ways:
our help comes from you.

Loving Father, we thank you
for your constant faithfulness to us
in spite of our tendency to fall far short
of our responsibilities.

Merciful Father,
accept these prayers
for the sake of your Son,
our Saviour Jesus Christ. Amen.

PROPER 25

When we recognise our dependence on God
we will approach him with true humility
and accept his gifts with joy.

Let us pray to the God who made us and sustains us.

Look with mercy on your Church,
with all our faults and failings,
missed opportunities and misunderstandings,
as we learn to be truly your body on earth.

Silence

God of our making:
have mercy on us.

We lay before you the political issues,
the moral dilemmas and the dreams of peace
that concern our world,
and all who share its resources.
Where we can see no clear way forward
give us your vision and enable us
to be good stewards of all you provide.

Silence

God of our making:
have mercy on us.

We ask you to take all our relationships
and drench them in your transforming love,
so that we appreciate one another more,
and value what each has to offer.

Silence

God of our making:
have mercy on us.

Surround with comfort and reassurance
those who feel spiritually dried-up
or emotionally drained;
heal and mend broken bodies and broken hearts,
and provide clear pools of water for those
who are walking the valley of misery and depression.

Silence

God of our making:
have mercy on us.

Gather into your kingdom
those who have run the race
and fought the good fight,
and have mercy on all who are at the point of death.

Silence

God of our making:
have mercy on us.

We give you thanks and praise
for the wideness of your mercy,
and the personal attention
of your provision for us.

Merciful Father,
accept these prayers
for the sake of your Son,
our Saviour Jesus Christ. Amen.

ALL SAINTS' DAY

In Christ we are chosen to be God's holy people.

Let us pray to the God
who can love sinners into saints.

Thank you, Father, for the faithful prayers
of so many over the generations;
for the lifetimes of quiet godliness;
for the struggles bravely borne
and the witness of strong faith.

Silence

Make us all:
worthy of our calling.

Thank you, Father, for all peace-makers
and those who strive for justice and reconciliation;
thank you for those who work to relieve suffering
and manage the world's resources more fairly.

Silence

Make us all:
worthy of our calling.

Thank you for the blessing and hope
of each new generation;
for the richness of good friendships,
the happiness of those in love,
and the comfort of prayer support.

Silence

Make us all:
worthy of our calling.

Thank you for the care and attention
given to those in pain and ill health;

for the example of those
whom it is always a pleasure to visit,
in spite of their suffering;
for those who allow their suffering
to be used for some good.

Silence

Make us all:
worthy of our calling.

Thank you for the love and encouragement
we have received through the years
from those who have died in faith
and are remembered with great affection.

Silence

Make us all:
worthy of our calling.

Thank you for all the saints of heaven
who join us as we praise God
in all his holiness.

Merciful Father,
accept these prayers
for the sake of your Son,
our Saviour Jesus Christ. Amen.

FOURTH SUNDAY BEFORE ADVENT

Jesus came to search out the lost and save them.
Through him we come to our senses and make our lives clean.

Let us still ourselves in our Father's presence
and tell him what is on our hearts.

Loving Father, look into us and teach us
to know ourselves more honestly,
to recognise the areas which need cleansing,
and rejoice in the work you have done
in our lives as individuals
and as the people of God.

Silence

Lord, may our lives:
express our love for you.

Fill Parliament and all places of government
throughout the world
with a desire for integrity and a determination
to stamp out corruption and deceit.
Guide all who lead and all who advise.

Silence

Lord, may our lives:
express our love for you.

Speak your peace and reconciliation
into all family disputes and hurtful misunderstandings;
nurture a spirit of loving community
in our neighbourhood,
and heighten our awareness of one another's needs.

Silence

Lord, may our lives:
express our love for you.

Bring reassurance and practical help
to those who are close to despair;
support those in long-term suffering
and use us as instruments of your healing love.

Silence

Lord, may our lives:
express our love for you.

Welcome into your kingdom
those who have faithfully lived out their days;
as we miss their physical presence,
we thank you for the gift of their lives.

Silence

Lord, may our lives:
express our love for you.

As today you have strengthened our resolve
to put our lives right with you,
we thank you for alerting us to dangers
and providing the courage to change.

Merciful Father,
accept these prayers
for the sake of your Son,
our Saviour Jesus Christ. Amen.

THIRD SUNDAY
BEFORE ADVENT

*Life after death is not wishful thinking
but a definite reality.*

Let us pray to the great God of heaven
who stands among us now.

Heavenly God, as the earthly part of your Church
we come before you with our thanks and praise
for your living presence among us,
in our worship together
and in our separate times of prayer.
We thank you for bringing the joy of heaven to earth
as you lift us into your presence.

Silence

You are our God:
living for ever and ever.

Look with mercy on our world
as we work out policies and target needs,
and misunderstand one another's cultures
and get carried away with excesses
and the taste of power.

Silence

You are our God:
living for ever and ever.

May our waking, working, eating, relaxing and sleeping
become a pattern coloured and lit by your love;
may our homes reflect it,
our places of work be energised by it,
and our relationships glow with it.

Silence

You are our God:
living for ever and ever.

To those who are losing heart
give your heavenly encouragement and patience;
to the young and vulnerable
give heavenly protection;
to the ill and the damaged
give heavenly healing and inner peace,
as you touch our lives with yours.

Silence

You are our God:
living for ever and ever.

Knowing that physical death
is not the end of life,
but the beginning of a new dimension,
we recall our loved ones who have died
and commend them to your eternal keeping.

Silence

You are our God:
living for ever and ever.

As you fill our hearts with heavenly joy
we pour out our love and praise
to you, our living God!

Merciful Father,
accept these prayers
for the sake of your Son,
our Saviour Jesus Christ. Amen.

SECOND SUNDAY
BEFORE ADVENT

*There will be dark and dangerous times as
the end approaches, but by standing firm
through it all we will gain life.*

The Lord is always ready to listen;
let us pray to him now.

Lord, we pray particularly for those
whose faith is being battered
and those who no longer pray;
we pray for our training programmes
and our weekly worship;
for our faith to be deepened and strengthened.

Silence

Keep us faithful:
firm to the end.

We pray for those whose responsibility it is
to manage the world's economy,
and for those who have difficult
ethical decisions to make;
we pray for wisdom and courage to do what is right.

Silence

Keep us faithful:
firm to the end.

We pray for the world our children will inherit
and ask your blessing on all parents
and the responsibilities they face;
we ask for understanding, maturity,
and the gift of laughter.

Silence

Keep us faithful:
firm to the end.

We pray for the victims of disasters,
famines, earthquakes and plagues;
for all who are crying
and those who have no tears left.
We pray for comfort, renewed strength,
and available friends.

Silence

Keep us faithful:
firm to the end.

We pray for those who are nearing death
and those who have died;
especially we pray for those
who have died suddenly and unprepared.
We pray for mercy and forgiveness.

Silence

Keep us faithful:
firm to the end.

We give you thanks, Lord God,
that you always provide the grace we need
to accomplish what you ask of us.

Merciful Father,
accept these prayers
for the sake of your Son,
our Saviour Jesus Christ. Amen.

CHRIST THE KING

This Jesus, dying by crucifixion between criminals,
is the anointed King of all creation
in whom all things are reconciled.

Through Jesus, our King, let us pray.

As we celebrate Jesus, the head of the Church body,
we pray for all the members
with their various gifts and ministries;
we pray that even our weaknesses
can be used to your glory
for the good of the world.

Silence

Christ is the image:
of the invisible God we worship.

May all monarchs and heads of state
be led in ways of truth and righteousness,
and recognise with humility
that they are called to serve.
We pray for all shepherds,
rescue teams and trouble-shooters;
for all who work to recover the lost.

Silence

Christ is the image:
of the invisible God we worship.

May we reach out to one another
with greater love and better understanding;
we pray for our homes, our relatives,
our neighbours and our friends,
particularly those who do not yet realise
the extent of your love for them.

Silence

Christ is the image:
of the invisible God we worship.

May those who have been scattered
far from their homes and loved ones
be enabled to live again in peace and happiness;
may the bitter and resentful find hope again
and the confused find new direction.

Silence

Christ is the image:
of the invisible God we worship.

May the dying know your closeness,
and those who mourn their loved ones
know for certain that your kingdom
stretches across both sides of death.

Silence

Christ is the image:
of the invisible God we worship.

Our hearts are filled with thanksgiving
as we realise again
the extraordinary extent of your love for us.

Merciful Father,
accept these prayers
for the sake of your Son,
our Saviour Jesus Christ. Amen.